D0522229

DEDICATION

I dedicate this book to my precious children, Kelvin, Andy Justyn and Olivia – thanks for being there through the hard days, believing with me, and showing me such love and care.

... and also to my loving Lord – thank you for giving me life and allowing me the privilege of sharing your hope with others.

"With long life will I satisfy her and show her my salvation." (Psalm 91:16)

ACKNOWLEDGMENTS

Special thanks to...
Andy for your expert help and advice in writing this book.
Kelvin for the Long Life Ministries website.
Justyn for your love, laptop, and sense of humour!
Olivia for being my very special princess.
My little grandson William for bringing me joy.
Rodney for your help writing my 'early days' and just for being my big
• *brother!*
Mum and Dad for being the best parents I could have.
Norma for your sisterly love.
William's Mum & Dad and sister Vie for love and prayers.
Malcolm & Liz for your constant love and support.
Wendy for always being there at any time.
Christine for being a friend indeed.
Wesley and Frances for being faith-filled encouragers.
Steven and Donna for standing with us on the Word.
Lara for the beauty of your song 'The Voice of Hope'
(and Donna, for first sharing it with me).
Alec & Maureen for being there in time of need.
Robert & Lorna, Cecil M., Ken & May, David & Ruth, Cecil & Evelyn,
William & Rosemary, Tom, Maggie & Andrew, Bella & Anthony, Joy,
Clifford & Ruth, Alison, Corwyn & Patricia, Meta, Michael & Esther, Millie,
Monica, June – for all you've done.
Bernie for your beautiful photos.
Pastor Justin for taking the time to care for us.
Tim Uluirewa whose worship leading brings us close to heaven.
Pastor Richard for inspiring me to pray for the sick.
Pastor Dave for believing God's healing power is for today and
encouraging me to share my story.
Paul Reid for words that influence, and Robin Mark for songs that inspire.
Aidan O'Brien for all your expert care and constant support.
Dr Kyle and all at Causeway Surgery.
Sam, Gillian, and the team at Ambassador for your patience and help well
beyond the call of duty!
All those who supported and encouraged me in any way, whether I have
managed to mention you in these pages or not.
And, finally, my husband William, without whom I could not have gone
through the most difficult days of my life - or written this book!

FOREWORD

I was sitting at my desk one Tuesday morning when my Community Pastor, Justin Marsh, phoned to tell me that Holy Trinity Brompton had recommended a Pastor and his wife from Newcastle, County Down to visit our Tuesday night 'Ministry of Power' service. I didn't know who they were or the seriousness of their situation. Since that call, and the visit they made that night with their daughter Olivia, William and Sharyn have become dear friends.

The story you will read will both excite and challenge you. This book not only walks you through a miraculous healing but allows you behind the scenery into their personal fears, questions and challenges. What thoughts go through your mind while you are waiting to die? What will happen to your husband and children? Yes, even Christians have to face these questions. The valley of the shadow of death is real, few walk it and come back, Sharyn did.

The many opportunities that have now opened up to them in the medical, media, community and Christian arena ARE truly amazing. Can Jesus Christ still do miracles? Read the book, one could happen for you!

Revd Dr David E Carr
Regional Overseer Free Methodist Church UK
Senior Pastor Renewal Christian Centre, Solihull, England

CONTENTS

1   PROLOGUE – NO PLAN 'B' 9
2   PARALLEL LIVES 12
3   REJOICE! 18
4   TAPESTRY 24
5   ALL THINGS WORK TOGETHER 30
6   FIRST TASTE OF FEAR 36
7   FORGET THE KITCHEN FLOOR! 41
8   'CHANCE' ENCOUNTERS 47
9   THE SILVER TEATRAY 52
10 THROUGH THE VALLEY 57
11 NEW LIFE - NEW FIGHT 63
12 NINETY-ONE 69
13 THE VOICE OF HOPE 74
14 BY HIS STRIPES 80
15 DIVINE APPOINTMENT 85

16 THE LONGEST DAY 91

PHOTOGRAPHS 97

17 DEATH IS NOT WELCOME HERE 105

18 AN ANGEL STOOD OVER ME 112

19 MY FAITH JACKET! 118

20 ONLY BELIEVE 123

21 NOT THAT I KNOW OF... 128

22 IT'S ONLY A NAME 133

23 RELEASED FROM CAPTIVITY 139

24 I HAVE MY LIFE BACK! 145

25 LIGHT THROUGH THE WINDOW 151

26 THE GREATEST MIRACLE 157

27 THESE SIGNS SHALL FOLLOW 163

28 SHOW ME! 170

29 ALL THINGS ARE POSSIBLE 179

30 ONE YEAR ON! 182

31 THE BEGINNING... 188

1

PROLOGUE - NO PLAN 'B'

It used to be that the 21st of June had only one meaning on the Mackay family calendar – it was my father-in-law's birthday. We would laugh and say to him, "Trust you to get the most out of your birthday by having it on the longest day of the year," for that's how it's known in my part of the world.

But the 21st of June 2004 was to be my longest day for a totally different reason. It was to be the day when I would be told the results of my latest scans. A day that would be a matter of life or death...

I waited with William in the room when the consultant came in with a nurse, sat down, and placed a file on the small table in front of us, his head bowed almost apologetically. He began to speak very quietly, so quietly that we strained to hear exactly what he was saying, not wanting to miss any detail of his prognosis.

"I'm here to talk about the management of your tumours," he began. I wondered what he meant by 'management'. Surely there was to be some course of treatment, some type of operation, some hope medically for my condition?

Slowly he shook his head, and explained that the cancer was deemed to be inoperable, and my condition was terminal. Treatment was unlikely to work, but even if it did, it would only add a couple of months, at most, to my life.

I tried to take in what he was saying. "A couple of months?" I said. "A couple of months onto what? How much time do I actually have?"

"I'll tell you if you really want to know," he replied. I felt somehow suspended in time. Lots of thoughts flashed through my mind in an instant. I wondered if he was talking in terms of years. Would I have time to see the children growing up? Would William and I see our next wedding anniversary? His next words would determine all of that. Did I really want to know the answer to my own question?

"Yes," I blurted out, almost involuntarily. "Yes, I want to know – how long do I have?"

"A year at the most," he said. "I'm sorry." His words cut through me like a knife. I collapsed into William's arms – I knew the news might not be good, but I had no idea that it would be quite this bad.

Later that evening William sent out an email to our friends who had been praying for us. It read...

22 June 2004, 02.27am

Dear friends

The specialist cancer consultant told us today that he would give Sharyn a year at the most to live, and that treatment is not a realistic option.

We believe that the Lord is on the throne, and that He can, and will, heal Sharyn, as her life is in His hands. Our God is the God of the impossible, and He alone can do it. We would really value your ongoing prayers at this time, as nothing short of a miracle will make a difference in this situation,

– That's Plan 'A', friends.

– There is no Plan 'B'...

2

PARALLEL LIVES

In these days Dublin, Ireland is a very cosmopolitan city, with a huge mixture of race, colour and creed. Like many capital cities it has a river which flows right through the middle of it, but there has always been more to it than that. The Liffey is almost like a border, a boundary whereby native Dubliners have always tended to define each other in terms of being a "Northsider" or a "Southsider". I suppose it's quite possible that some people have lived most of their lives without ever venturing from one side into the other!

I was a "Southsider", William a "Northsider", and for our first few years we managed to live what we have often referred to as "parallel lives!"

William was the first to arrive on the scene, born in the Rotunda Hospital Dublin, on the 7th of June 1961. He lived on the Northside of Dublin with his Mum and Dad, Emily and Bobby Mackay, his older brother Robin, and his sister Vie. His mum had always said that if she was blessed with another boy, she would name him after her father, and ten years after Vie was born, she got her wish!

It was a happy childhood, and he attended both North Strand Church of Ireland and the primary school that nestled next to it, not too far from his home. He went along to Boys Brigade from a very young age, and just before he was due to go into secondary school, the family moved home to be nearer to his dad's work.

In the first of some interesting parallels in our lives, a little girl was born into the Croly family on the south side of Dublin, nine months later, almost to the day.

There are two things that everyone in my family remembers about the first day of March 1962. One is that I was born, and the other is that it was snowing at the time!

I too had a couple of older siblings, making me very much the baby of the family. My sister Norma went around proudly announcing to everyone who would listen that she had a baby sister, whereas my brother Rodney being a typical boy, arrived at the nursing home with the words, "Well, where is it?!"

My parents Jim and Betty Croly had lived in Canada for some time before returning to Dublin, and Norma had always said that if I turned out to be a girl she wanted me to be named after her best friend in Vancouver. Thus I entered the world with the name 'Sharyn' spelled the Canadian way – *with a 'Y!'* I can't think of how many times in my life I've had to add that three-word phrase when I have given my name, whether in school, or work, or ministry. I like my name, but I also like people to spell it correctly!

My mother had an unusual maiden name – Linnau, which came from my Austrian grandfather. He had moved some years before from Austria to a small island in the Irish Sea called the Isle of Man. Although she and dad had lived in Dublin and then Greystones, County Wicklow for many years, she is always proud to call herself Manx. The Island was a place we went to visit often when I was growing up, as did William with his family. Recently we discovered that we had both kept a hymn sheet for the Kirk Bradden open air service dated the same Sunday, many years before we actually met!

I've always been very close to Norma and Rodney, and my brother was somewhat of an Action Man! I can remember him building a boat, learning to fly, and more recently, with his wife, Sylvia becoming very proficient both at alpine skiing and sailing. It may have been something to do with being born on a snowy day, but when I was growing up, one of my favourite things to do was to go up the Dublin Mountains in the winter with him, and his trusty sledge. One of those times he launched me down a hill at breakneck speed and I hit a hidden log, which catapulted me through the air. Even though I was fourteen years old, I was still very much my mum and dad's 'little girl', so we conspired not to divulge the details of this particular near-death experience to them!

William's brother had been to Mountjoy and Marine school, and the year that he started it had been renamed and re-classified as Mount Temple Comprehensive. He has always maintained that it was one of the most progressive schools of its day, and some of his teachers such as Donald Moxham, Albert Bradshaw, and Jack Heaslip helped to create an ethos which very much encouraged pupils to be individuals in life. It was an atmosphere too where the Christian Union began to thrive, although he wasn't a part of it for some time.

My home was in Terenure and I attended Grosvenor Road Baptist Church with my family, went to Rathgar National Primary School, and then went to The High School, also in Rathgar. Although I usually cycled there, as the 'little girl' of the family, my dad always spoiled me, driving me to school when it rained, something he continued to do even when I was finished school and working!

One day William's Religious Education teacher, Sophie Shirley, announced that there was to be a debate about the truth of the resurrection. William took up the challenge to speak for it, and won the debate. A man who had been sitting in at the back of the class came up to him and announced himself as Joe Fudge, from the Don Summers Crusade which was holding meetings in the YMCA. Based on William's apparent mastery of biblical truth, he wanted to know if he would like to join the team of counsellors at the Youth Event later in the week!

Of course, his head knowledge had been gleaned from some good books for the purpose of winning a debate and he had no idea what this man was talking about! Joe quickly realised that, and instead invited William to come along to the youth event and bring some friends. The meeting would be held on the 22nd of November 1974, and most of his friends decided to go along to see what this was all about.

He was just on his way out through the door when he realised that there was something on the TV he wanted to see, perhaps Manchester United in a European Cup match. Whatever it was, he stayed put, and his school friends all went to the meeting, and what's more – they all went forward to give their hearts to Christ!

A while ago I was looking through my 'keepsake' box and came across a small pink card which was headed The Don Summers Crusade – My Personal Decision ... it was signed *Sharyn B. Croly, 22/11/74*. I had gone along with the Youth Club from my church that same evening, and had made a commitment to follow the Lord at exactly the same time as William's friends! The next day in my school I had such a sense of peace knowing that I had taken a big step that night that would affect my life for years to come.

Over at his school William didn't know what had hit him! Suddenly all his friends had become Christians and they were rather keen that he should become one too! It took some time until he met with singer/evangelist Dave Pope on a weekend away, who led him to the Lord. All this time, word was circulating that something very special was happening in Mount Temple School. Morning and lunchtime meetings were crammed with pupils wanting to come together for prayer and worship – it was nothing short of a mini revival!

One place that defied the Northside/Southside 'divide' was Dublin's YMCA. Young Christians from all over the city came together on Saturday evenings for the Y Club and on Sunday evenings for a large after-church service called The 8.30, followed by coffee in Jonathans restaurant in Grafton Street, which reserved a section especially for us! William and I had been there with mutual friends on numerous occasions before we actually met up with each other.

Girls' Brigade played a big part in my life as well, and one of the folks I got to know at the district officer's training sessions was a really nice girl called Alison Stewart, who went to the same school as William; in fact, they were both prefects there, and so knew each other very well.

It was at this time that William developed a friendship that has lasted for many years, well beyond school. Alison's boyfriend was a chap called Paul Hewson and he was working with three other guys, Larry, Adam and Dave in a band that Larry had put together originally by putting up a note on their school noticeboard.

William clearly recalls one day when they sat down together, and he said, 'Things are going well, we've got a new manager called Paul, and he said we need a new name, so there it is." William looked at what he had written on a piece of paper, and said, "U2 – What kind of name is that?!" Bono, which was his generally accepted name by then, laughed, "Well, we'll all have to get used to it!" he said. William replied, "Well, you've got a great sound, but I just hope a name like that catches on." I think it would be fair to say that it did!

William recalls a time in Maths class, (which was not by any means his favourite subject), when the teacher showed them two lines running along a large board. "What do you call these?" asked Mr Maxwell. "Parallel lines, sir?" ventured William. "Ah well, they may appear that way," he said, "but look at this." He proceeded to remove the piece of card that was covering the rest of the board and, much to their surprise, the two lines met at the end. "It only takes the most gradual change of direction along the way," he said, "and two lines will meet with each other, no matter how they look at the start of the picture."

When I look back now, I can see how those gradual changes would put our seemingly parallel lives firmly on course, not only to meet together, but to stay together for many years to come.

3

REJOICE!

When William left school he went to work in Dublin Tourism, and then secured a job in Thomas Cook Travel, which he would begin following the October Bank Holiday weekend of 1978. I still had another year to complete in The High School, but a small change of plan and direction meant our paths were about to cross. Robbie, who was a mutual friend of both myself and William, invited him to come on a Y Club weekend. He hadn't been to the Y for a few weeks at that time, whereas I was a regular attender.

Reluctantly he agreed to come along, and that Friday evening we were all on the top deck of the bus heading to Greystones. He at the front, I down at the back. I wandered up to the front and turned to have a conversation with Robbie, and that's when William spotted me! You may not believe in love at first sight – but William insists that it does exist, and he immediately set about trying to find out who I was, and if I was 'attached!' Over that weekend we developed a friendship, which we both knew was a lot deeper than a casual one. I have to admit that there were a couple of other guys who seemed overly interested in me, but I had just split up with my boyfriend, and really wasn't interested in them. However, I really enjoyed William's company, and the weekend finished all too quickly for both of us.

The day after the weekend William started in his new job as a travel agent, and I went back to school, wondering when I might see him again. Then the most peculiar thing happened, I got called out of my class to go to the school office and there I was given a telephone number to ring. "It sounds quite important," they said.

I called the number and it was William! "I wasn't sure how to get hold of you," he said. Then he came up with his big proposal, "Would you like to learn how to play the guitar?!" He told me later that he didn't want to take a chance on waiting until the next weekend, just in case the other boys had a chance to ask me out, so he had to think of some excuse to call me. I have to hand it to him – it was an unusual chat-up line!

I agreed to meet up with him that Saturday to begin my 'guitar lessons'. When I arrived at his home his parents had gone out and he offered to make me a cup of coffee, 'the special way my mum makes them'. Unfortunately, he forgot to take the centre part out of the blender lid, and as soon as it was switched on, the pressure caused it to practically explode, as the lid blew off, and the coffee went everywhere! It wasn't exactly the most impressive start to the day as we cleaned up the mess!

The guitar lessons were a much better option, although we spent more time talking than playing. I had only learned about six chords, the same six chords I know today, when William leaned over and kissed me. Later that evening we walked into the Y Club hand in hand so everyone could see we were together, and we have been ever since.

I still say that he had to come over to the Southside to get the right girl! My parents subtly asked my brother to check out this Northsider, but as he already knew William's sister Vie, he confirmed to them that they had nothing to worry about!

Our love continued to deepen and grow over the following years. When I finished in school, I became a legal secretary, and worked very near to Dublin's Four Courts. William's office in Thomas Cook was at the end of Grafton Street, so we would meet halfway at the famous Ha'penny Bridge and go to lunch together almost every day.

We announced our engagement at William's 21st Birthday party, and then married just under a year later on 16th May 1983, followed by a lovely honeymoon in Singapore and Penang, where we were upgraded to first class thanks to our lovely friends in Singapore Airlines!

Our first son Kelvin was born the following year on 29th July and Andy, a couple of years later, also in July.

Life was busy with two small children under the age of three. We continued to walk with the Lord, being involved in both Grosvenor Road Baptist Church and Kingdom Life Fellowship, with most of our Y Club friends.

We moved to Bray, County Wicklow in 1988, and shortly afterwards William was approached by the local Methodist and Church of Ireland Ministers to ask if he would consider becoming the Boys Brigade captain.

We talked and prayed about it, and together felt that it was the right thing to do. Part of the object of the BB is "... *the advancement of Christ's Kingdom among boys*". It seemed like a wonderful opportunity to ensure that our company fulfilled that ethos amongst the 70 boys who attended, from Junior to Senior level, including our own.

Just before the season began, William had organised an officers meeting at our home. We were just about to start when the doorbell rang, and I went to answer it. I'd never seen the man who was standing there before, so he said with a broad smile, "Hello, I'm the new Methodist minister, is this where the BB meeting is?" I invited him in and he introduced himself as Stewart Morris, our new BB chaplain. It was our first meeting, and we've remained close friends ever since.

Justyn had been born the previous year, and we wanted to get involved in a church that was more local to us. Because of our new connection through the BB and Stewart, we decided to start attending Bray Methodist Church. The first Sunday that we went it was by far the coldest day of the year! It was snowing heavily and there was hardly a car to be seen on the road. Even though the congregation was depleted in numbers by the freezing weather, we had a wonderfully warm welcome by the ladies there, Heather Brown, Heather Gandola and June Glascott, who took it in turns over the following weeks to take baby Justyn off my hands so that I could concentrate on the service.

After a while, and with Stewart's encouragement, William's ministry began to increase in the church. We began a monthly Sunday evening contemporary worship service for all ages called Bray Praise. Another friend, Rosemary Lindsay, had just begun studying for her accreditation as a Local Preacher, and Stewart suggested that it would be good for William to do this too. So they both began to take services and go to classes over the next year or so, until they were fully qualified.

During this time William was asked whether he would consider coming to work fulltime for the Methodist Church, and so it was that we moved to North County Dublin, to live in Swords – yes, this Southsider temporarily became an honorary Northsider!

For the next three years William worked as a Lay Assistant to Rev Dudley Levistone Cooney in a circuit of three churches, taking services, pastoral visiting, and trying to establish some local work in Swords.

He was also the Dublin District Youth Secretary, charged with coming up with innovative ideas for reaching young people with the gospel. As a model Bray Praise was working very well, but we wanted to develop it into a city-wide event, with a name that captured the essence of what we were trying to achieve. Thus Rejoice! began, a large event of praise, worship and drama which took place monthly, alternating on either side of Dublin.

One day I suggested that we should do something similar to bring the gospel to children, and so Rejoice for Kids! was born, with lots of drama, children's music, and even puppets made a regular contribution. As chairman of the Irish Methodist Association of Youth Clubs William introduced Rejoice! to become the main worship part of the IMAYC weekend, and it helped to provide a platform for what is now the annual Autumn Soul weekend as it prompted us to understand that young people may love sports, but they also love to get to grips with the reality of the gospel too.

We travelled around the country with Rejoice on the Road! encouraging churches to run similar events locally. All of these things were used by the Lord to reach out to people with the gospel, and that was at the heart of our ministry. We worked together in planning them, although I managed, with great effort, to stay firmly in the background. I'm just not an 'up-front' kind of person I reasoned, and I didn't think that I ever would be.

Although we were very committed to the whole idea of renewing worship and praise, we also realised that there needed to be a balance in terms of meeting physical as well as spiritual needs, mainly because of reading these words in Amos 5:23-24:

"Take away from me the noise of thy songs ... let justice roll down as waters, and mercy as a mighty stream."

We began to get heavily involved in the Fair Trade campaign, encouraging Churches to use and shops to sell their tea, coffee and other goods at a time when they really didn't want to know. William even managed to persuade the Irish Minister for Social Welfare, Dr Michael Woods, to come along and address a meeting we organised to promote the campaign. As the response to this idea began to grow, we got involved with a further development of seeking justice with yet another unpopular idea at the time – Third World Debt cancellation. In these days it's good to see how far up the political agenda these things have moved, and how many mainstream shops carry Fair Trade stock. We're blessed when we look back and see how many principles of justice straight from the Word of God are applied to everyday life now, even if they were a long time coming!

We lived in Swords for three years, and through that time, with Dudley's enthusiastic support and encouragement, William went through the long process of candidature and was accepted for the Methodist Ministry, which meant going for ministerial training to Edgehill College/Queens University, Belfast.

As a family, it meant that we were on the move again, with all the changes to home and school that this entailed, but we were trusting that God had opened the door, and we sought His help as we ventured to go through it.

4

TAPESTRY

For the three years that William was engaged in his ministerial studies we lived in Bangor, County Down. The family went along to Wesley Centenary Methodist Church on Hamilton Road, where he was also on placement as an assistant to a minister who would become one of our dearest friends, Rev Trevor Kennedy.

During that time a new course was introduced into the church by Trevor. He said it was called Alpha and he needed some volunteers to lead some groups. There were no 'experts' or 'advisers' around at that time, so he said that as we were all 'equally ignorant' we would watch some training videos and, hopefully, it would all work out!

As William was tied up with assignments for college on most weeknight evenings, I agreed to go along, just to find out how it worked. However, Trevor can be very persuasive, and I found myself jointly leading a group, even though as a leader I didn't know much more than the participants. We all managed to get through it and be blessed by it, and I shared with William that I felt this was something we could get more involved with in the future. When the next course came along, however, I was able to attend everything except the Alpha dinner. I was otherwise occupied; in fact, I was in hospital shortly after having a baby!

On the 20th of June 1997 we went to the annual close of year prize-giving event in Kilmaine Primary School. We knew that Andy was going to be receiving one of the major awards and, therefore, it would be at the end of the evening. Suddenly I started to feel some pains and knew it was the beginning of labour; however, I didn't want to miss seeing Andy getting his prize, so I hung on! When it was over we dashed back to the house and called up a friend from the church whom we had pre-arranged would come over and look after the boys in case this should happen. The only problem was that when I rang Edith and said, "It's time for the new arrival, can you come over right away?" She said, "Oh dear, my daughter has taken the car, but you're not due for another week yet, are you?"

She was right! All the boys had been a week or two late when they arrived, and now this baby was coming earlier than the due date, but she did promise to get over as soon as she could. I had visions of having to give birth to my baby at home, in the car, or in the hospital car park! It turned out that Edith couldn't contact her daughter, so she called Trevor and he jumped in his car right away to bring her to my house. As they drove at some pace around the ring road to our house, Edith felt that Trevor wasn't driving fast enough, and enquired whether he as a minister had ever had any training about delivering babies! "Absolutely not!" he replied. "In that case, do what you are good at and pray that we get there on time!"

Her words had the desired effect, and very quickly they pulled up outside our home with a wave, as we took off at speed to Belfast's Jubilee Maternity Hospital where our beautiful baby Olivia was born. I couldn't have been happier that night as my dream of someday having a daughter had come true. The future was looking bright as I held my Bangor baby in my arms.

A few months later, on 30th August 1997, we were watching TV when the shocking news came through that the Princess of Wales had been involved in a serious car accident in Paris, but first reports were hopeful. As the night progressed it was announced that the accident had been a fatal one, and the Princess had died. William was taking the service the next morning entirely on his own for the first time, and had planned it to be a fairly 'upbeat' occasion ... Now the nation was in shock, mourning their Princess, so William stayed up most of the night re-planning the service to make it more suitable to reflect the sense of loss that was evident throughout the whole country.

At the same time baby Olivia had not been very well and as the week went on she became very ill indeed. On the day of Princess Diana's funeral, she was admitted to Dundonald Hospital for tests, where her condition gave cause for great concern. William cancelled a planned trip to a conference in Dublin and I was given a room in the hospital so that I could stay by her bedside constantly. During that time Trevor Kennedy was a wonderful source of strength to us, visiting at all hours of the day and night.

One day a nurse came in with some soft toys. The boys picked out a beautiful basket with a large red ribbon around it and a white teddy bear sitting inside, which they placed at the end of Olivia's cot. "It was left at Stormont with thousands of others in memory of Princes Diana," she said.

We are grateful to the hospital and to the Lord that Olivia fully recovered from that illness, and to this day she treasures her Princess Di Teddy.

At the end of the three years William graduated with an honours degree in theology from Queens, and was ordained at the Methodist Conference in Cork in June 1999.

A couple of weeks later we were settling into our manse on the Charlemont and Cranagill circuit of five churches, on the Portadown to Moy road. It was a lovely place, surrounded by apple trees, in what is referred to as Orchard County. Kelvin transferred from Methody to our nearest grammar school, the Royal School Dungannon, and Andy went into first year there at the same time.

It was during this time that I made some of my closest friends among the girls at our midweek morning Bible study, in particular, Millie, Iris, Glynis, and my dearest friends Wendy and Christine who attended our Blackwatertown church.

One day our society steward, who also ran the Bowls Club, came to tell us that his son was going into hospital for a serious kidney operation, so William went to visit him in the Urology Department of Craigavon Area Hospital. The procedure was a great success and it was decided that, at the next opportunity, the Bowls Club would raise some funds for the department. One evening we arranged to present the cheque when the local press came to photograph the Senior Consultant receiving it.

As he accepted the cheque, he told us a little about the fine work that the Department of Urology did, and continues to do, thanking all who had contributed and finishing with the words, "You never know when one of you might be the one who needs us in the future!"

I looked around at the older folk gathered there and wondered which of them might need the services of that department. As I was chatting to my good friend Gloria, I noticed the consultant on his own with a cup of tea, so I went over to thank him for finding the time in his busy schedule to come and receive the cheque personally. I introduced myself to him and we were talking for a while when the press photographer came over to check our names, "Mrs Mackay, isn't it?" he said, "and your name, sir?" "I'm Aidan O'Brien," he said. I again thanked him as he finished his tea and left for home, not really expecting to see him again. How wrong I would prove to be!

The three years on our first circuit passed fairly quickly and we found ourselves moving again, this time into the centre of Portadown, to take up the reins in three churches there. It wasn't very long before William struck up a really good friendship with the pianist and BB captain in our Epworth Church, David Blevins. With his job as one of the main correspondents in Ireland for Sky News, David would often be out of town, and that could be anywhere from West Cork to Washington. However, when he was available, they loved to lead worship together, which was really anointed by the Lord, and a real blessing to others. Of course, they also managed to drink large amounts of coffee late into the night, putting the world to right, as I would comment. And they say that women can talk!

We started to consider whether we should try to run an Alpha Course in Portadown, but we wanted it be one that would draw people in from all sides of the community, and not just our own congregations. One day William was visiting with a dear old lady called Mrs Troughton, from our Battlehill church, who was always a joy to meet. She was a woman who told us that she prayed constantly for "souls to be saved". This day her son and his wife, Terry and Maureen, were visiting with her too, and when they heard of our vision for Alpha, really encouraged us to pursue it, and not to be distracted from it, for they were sure the Lord was in it. They had been running Alpha for a number of years themselves in their Presbyterian church in Bangor.

With that encouragement we went ahead and set it all up, and it had a tremendous response. We saw the Lord working through the course in a mighty way, and many new friendships were developed, as people with very different backgrounds started to get to know each other. A number of the folks attending began committing and re-committing their lives to Christ, and we praised God for his faithfulness as people responded to the truth of the gospel.

We were appointed as Alpha Regional Advisers by Holy Trinity, Brompton which led to us organising the first Regional Alpha Day in Ireland, to encourage leaders or potential Alpha leaders from all over the country. HTB sent a team over to do the training, which included two people who would also become good friends, Gillian Lindsay who had come to the Lord during the ITV series "Alpha – Will it change their lives?" and Inger Lannero, who was responsible for co-ordinating all of the regional Alpha Advisers. The day was a great success, resulting in the establishment of several new Regional Advisers, and we eventually formed a national co-ordinating team.

I once heard somebody describe life as a tapestry, not unlike one that we have hanging on the wall in our home. Look at the back and all you can see is a seemingly unrelated series of tangled threads, loose ends, unravelled knots and unrelated colours. Look on the other side and you have a beautiful vibrant picture, when the pattern has developed and all those tangled threads hold a completely different meaning.

A verse in Proverbs says much the same thing ...

"Many are the plans in a man's heart, but it is the Lord's purpose that prevails." (Proverbs 19:21)

The time came for us to follow another of those tangled threads in our lives as we were to be on the move again, from Portadown to another circuit. We just had to trust the Lord, that he could see the bigger picture, the other side of the tapestry.

5

ALL THINGS WORK TOGETHER ...

It was at this time of anticipation and change that life was to take a turn which we never could have expected. William is a long-standing Manchester United fan, man and boy as they say, so as usual when we fancied a break the first thing he would reach for was not the computer, or a travel brochure, but the home fixture list to check out if United had a match at Old Trafford!

Of course, there is a major compensation for me – the Trafford Centre! A very large shopping mall just outside Manchester that's more than that – restaurants, shops, cinemas, kids play areas, and a unique ambience all designed to make you feel that you're not really shopping at all, but enjoying a lovely day out. At least that's the way I see it! Some people will never understand why I like to go there, but then I don't understand why they don't! Thank the Lord that He made us all different, but I've definitely got that 'good eye for a quality bargain' gene built into me somewhere. I suspect that the ladies reading this might understand what I'm talking about better than the men! Thankfully, I'm blessed with a husband who quite likes it too, but not least because it's got a great Starbucks, which allows him to escape from the serious business of shopping!

It was Easter 2003, and we had made our bookings, and were all set to travel after the usual round of Holy Week and Easter Services which William either conducted or in which he played a part. Our good friends Dave and Jane Martin lived in Manchester, Dave being the minister of Cheadle Hulme Methodist Church. He worked with the Methodist evangelist Rob Frost, organising an event called Easter People and William had played in the worship band there. For the last couple of years we hadn't actually gone to the event, but when they were there we stayed in their home - a sort of 'half manse swop!' It was an arrangement that worked well, and we were looking forward to the break.

However, it was during the week leading up to Easter that I began to experience sharp pains in my lower abdomen, pains that got more severe by the day. On the Easter Bank Holiday Monday we decided to contact the doctor-on-call, and on hearing the symptoms over the telephone they told me to come over right away. A very pleasant doctor checked me over and quickly reached a conclusion. "Suspected appendicitis" was his prognosis, and within a couple of hours I found myself being examined in the A&E department of Craigavon Area Hospital. They agreed with the doctor-on-call's reading of the situation, and I was admitted that evening, hoping upon hope that all would be clear and that it wouldn't put our travel plans in jeopardy. Maybe we would still make it to Manchester. As it happened, missing our Easter break would prove to be a very minor problem indeed.

The hospital carried out a number of their usual procedures. After a while the "appendix" pain seemed to gradually subside. However, investigations and an ultrasound scan had revealed what appeared to be a large cyst on my kidney. The news came totally unexpected, but it was suggested to me that this was not an uncommon occurrence and perhaps I should just go home and forget about it. When I was discussing this with William, he suddenly remembered that he knew a Senior Consultant in the Department of Urology, Aidan O'Brien, the same man I had met and chatted with a few years before in Cranagill.

He's a very busy man who not only works in Craigavon Hospital, but also has a worldwide reputation for excellence and is frequently in demand as a conference speaker. William didn't mention where he was going to me at that time, in case he wasn't available and I would be disappointed, but as it happened, and much to his surprise, he was not only in the building, but in his office! We later found out that he was actually travelling to the USA the following day to present a paper – God's timing is perfect!

When William went to find out whether Aidan was about, he tapped on a door which said Department of Urology - Mr O'Brien's Secretary. "Come on in," came the voice from inside, and with some trepidation, he put his head around the door. There, surrounded by seemingly endless files, for the first time he met Monica, a delightful lady who completely puts the lie to the notion that Doctor's secretaries are dragons waiting to pounce on you, should you ask for anything out of the ordinary!

With a pleasant smile she informed William that Mr O'Brien was in his office on a call, but if he waited, she was sure he would have a word. Since that original meeting at the fund-raiser, William had encountered Aidan a number of times while visiting members of his congregation and when acting as hospital Chaplain. In fact, he had been chatting to him just a few months earlier at the staff Christmas party, so they were not total strangers. Having exchanged greetings he said that he would be happy to take a look over my file before he went away, and would then assign some of his staff to keep an eye on my case if he felt it was appropriate. It's amazing how things work out in life, or should I say how God works things out, for at this time neither of them could have imagined just how much that brief conversation would impact upon our lives over the next year and a half.

William came back into the ward with a big smile on his face and shortly after that the sign on my bed was changed to read, Urology – Mr O'Brien. Aidan came to see me in my hospital bed later that day and advised me that I could be discharged after a couple of days. He would examine my file fully on his return from America, and Monica would contact me with an appointment to review my case.

I remembered the evening when he had said, "You never know when you might be the one who needs us in the future!" As I reflected on his words, I realised that I had never thought that one just might turn out to be me.

I left the hospital looking forward to our hastily re-arranged break, and confident that I was in the best of hands, medically speaking, but we were oblivious to what was to come.

Some years ago when William first became a Christian as a teenager, he had 'adopted' a verse which he would always add to his signature – 'Romans chapter 8, verse 28:

> *"And we know that all things work together for good to those who love God, to those who are called according to his purpose."*

His mother happened to notice it and said, "That's a great verse to live by, but it's a challenging one too, and the day will come when you'll have a chance to prove whether you really believe that it's true." It seemed to William that the time had arrived, and his belief in the truth of that verse would certainly be put to the test over the following year.

During the next couple of months we tried our best to put all the medical details out of our minds and set about preparing for our move to Newcastle, getting packed up, and checking out a Primary School for Olivia and a Grammar School for Justyn, who was at that time in the Royal School, Dungannon. Andy was there too and was just coming up to his GCSE exams. He was now 16 and had been in RSD from first year, and there was no way he wanted to move away from his friends, his academic achievements to date, and his rugby! Of course, he assured us that the family came a very close second!

We looked at a few possibilities for Andy when David Blevin's mother, who was a pastoral visitor in our Epworth Methodist congregation, stepped in with an offer that was a real blessing. She had run a Bed and Breakfast in her lovely home for many years, and had decided to retire from it. When she heard how Andy wanted to stay in his school, she explained that she would now have a couple of rooms free, and offered that Andy could lodge with her, and David's sister, Ruth. He would come home to Newcastle after rugby on a Saturday, and at term breaks. This meant that it was possible for him to continue through in RSD to become a prefect/deputy head-boy and achieve great A-level results.

Maureen Blevins was like a second mum to him, and is a real woman of God. Every Monday evening she holds meetings in her home when the praise and worship can be LOUD! We would laugh when Andy said there was no escape from hearing God's Word, even if he wanted to!

Things seemed to be working out fine as Justyn got good results and a place at Down High in Downpatrick, the nearest Grammar school to the new manse, and Olivia was to move to Newcastle Primary School. A letter arrived from Craigavon Area Hospital confirming that my appointment had been made for

June and, in the midst of packing up to move, we went to see Mr O'Brien to discuss what, if anything, was to be done about this cyst on my kidney.

He asked me whether there was still any pain or discomfort, and when I said that I was still experiencing back and other pain, he decided there and then that the best course of action was to bring me into hospital just before the children started back to school. Arrangements were made for me to attend for a couple of days stay in August to drain the cyst – a relatively simple and routine procedure ... nothing at all to worry about, or so we thought.

6

FIRST TASTE OF FEAR

We moved to Newcastle, County Down at the beginning of July and set about getting settled into a new circuit of three churches. Two of them were in the seaside towns of Newcastle and Dundrum, and the third in the historic town of Downpatrick, not far from the ancient church of Saul, the oldest church in Ireland which was founded by Saint Patrick, after whom the town was named.

In a large town like Portadown, the summer tended to see things get a little quieter as a lot of organisations and meetings closed down for the holiday season. Dundrum and Newcastle, however, were very much holiday resorts, and therefore a hive of activity during the summer months. It was a question of "hitting the ground running" and getting to grips with things from day one! It wasn't that this was a bad thing for we always regarded the fact that so many people came in the summer meant that we were really well placed for outreach and evangelism; we started shaping up plans to address what William called "this window of opportunity".

The first thing we noticed was that there were lots of visitors there every Sunday, many of whom were on holiday from our previous churches – no chance for William to re-use his old sermons here then! There were Sunday morning worship services and then a late Epilogue service that had been running on Sunday evenings each July and August in Newcastle. It was designed in such a way that holidaymakers who might have been away down the coast, or spent the day on the beach could come along, sing praise, and hear the gospel clearly preached. William called it The 8.30! for a number of reasons. One was that it reminded us of the meeting with the same name that used to be held in the YMCA in Dublin when we were teenagers, another was simply that it helped people to remember what time it was on!

However, the main reason was that it didn't have a standard service format and was open to whatever changes he felt led to make, especially introducing new songs of worship. There was a husband and wife team in Newcastle – Corwyn and Patricia, she played the organ in the morning and he the piano in the evening. William would often tell a joke that was doing the "ministerial rounds" at the time – "What's the difference between an organist and a terrorist?" – "Well, you can negotiate with a terrorist!" Of course, the reason why I can write this here is that nothing could be further from the truth when it came to this couple. They graciously overlooked William's propensity to give in his hymns a little bit later than was "officially acceptable", and Corwyn was only too willing to learn new songs which he and William would teach on Sunday evenings, alongside playing some more traditional hymns. At that time we had no idea of the part the availability and flexibility of The 8.30 would play in establishing our future ministry.

So it was that most of July and August was spent getting to grips with a new area, new people, and a new ministry. Although we had changed regions now, we were appointed Alpha Advisers for the South Down area, and set about helping some churches along the coast who were working together to prepare their courses to coincide with the annual Alpha Invitation in September. We planned to hold the Prayer Initiative evening in our church and William set about making some contacts with some of the other clergy in Newcastle, with a view to the possibility of running a town-wide Alpha course with them the following year.

The time for my planned short hospital stay drew nearer, but it was just a date in the diary at that time, something to get done and dusted without any great fuss. We were in the midst of change, but totally unprepared for what would happen next – that seemingly routine stay in hospital was to totally change our lives.

I checked into the hospital at the end of August, and following the usual preparations and procedures settled down for the night. The next day I was brought down to theatre. I had been told that draining the cyst should only take about twenty minutes or so under a local anaesthetic. Although its effects made me quite drowsy, I was still awake enough to watch the hands of a clock on the theatre wall moving slowly around. It began to occur to me that something was not quite right when the expected twenty minute procedure stretched to close on an hour and a half. I felt that something was definitely not going as planned, but I didn't know what. It appeared that the procedure had not worked as expected.

I was then told that they hadn't been able to drain the cyst. Shortly after I was wheeled back up to the ward.

I was lying there wondering what the next step was going to be when a nurse came alongside my hospital bed and said I would not be going through that procedure again, and instead had been scheduled to have a scan the following morning.

Later on that evening the nurses' shift changed and I was delighted to see who came on for night duty. Millie is a senior nurse who used to attend our weekly midweek ladies morning meeting when we lived in Cranagill. It was so nice to have the re-assurance of a familiar smile and chat from time to time as she went about the ward.

The next day started off like any other in hospital, and I was still hoping to get home as planned. William had a prior commitment in Dundrum at lunchtime and would come across to see me when he had finished. We had no reason at that time to believe that all these procedures were anything but routine.

I was brought to the scanning room, and the team there suggested that I should try to relax, because it wouldn't take long. "That's easy for you to say!" I thought as they disappeared behind the screen, leaving me with only the scanner for company. The scan ran its course and I lay on the table in the scanning room assuming that I would now be brought straight back up to the ward. Then the radiographer came over to me with a fairly grim look on his face – it was the sort of look that was to become very familiar to me as it was to appear on the faces of many doctors and consultants in the following months.

He told me that the scan had shown them that it was not a cyst on my kidney as first believed, but it was in fact a large tumour. He couldn't or wouldn't tell me any more there and then, I would have to wait and see my consultant to find out what he had to say.

This news was as shocking as it was unexpected. I could hardly take it in. I felt numb. That word "tumour" was one I had never expected to hear, and in my mind could only mean one thing. I didn't even want to think about that. A deep sense of anxiety flooded over me. I couldn't think of anything to say, instead I burst into tears.

A nurse came and held my hand while they waited to take me back to my bed, I just wanted to call William, but unfortunately when I did get to a phone his mobile was out of range, so I rang my sister in Dublin and she tried to console me. "Just because it's a tumour doesn't mean it's malignant," she said. I hoped with all my heart that she was right, but it wouldn't be the last time that I would speak to her from my hospital bed with bad news. After a while I managed to contact William who dropped everything and drove the hour and a half that it was from our manse to the hospital. Mr O'Brien had arrived and I felt somewhat re-assured by his calming presence beside my bed. However, there was no getting away from the fact that, following some discussion with him, the decision was taken that I should have a few more procedures over the next few days and then sent home to await an appointment to have surgery, probably in about three to five weeks time.

The object of the surgery would be to remove the tumour, preferably leaving the kidney intact. A biopsy would be carried out on it and, hopefully, it would prove to be benign. At that point the "C" word was never used, but it loomed in the back of my mind … what if? – I tried not to think about it too much, but hospital nights can be long and drawn out, with far too much thinking time available. Sleep didn't come easily that evening. As I thought over the events of the day, I realised that I had just my first real taste of fear.

7

FORGET THE KITCHEN FLOOR!

A few more days passed and I became more hopeful that when the time of the operation came the chances were very good that the tumour would come away from the kidney and that the kidney would be able to stay put. However, in the event that it did have to be removed, I was assured that it is possible to live a full and normal life with just one kidney, and many people are walking around just like that. I have to admit that even with that information, I still hoped it would be in place when I woke up after the surgery, but then that was weeks away anyway, wasn't it? The answer was a resounding NO!

The day came when I was due to go home. I was looking forward to seeing Justyn and Olivia in their new school uniforms and thinking about getting back to some sort of normality when Aidan O'Brien walked over to my bed accompanied by a nurse. He asked me how I was feeling and I said that I was looking forward to getting home. He then told me that he had just had a cancellation and could do my operation that very day – if I agreed to it.

It was completely out of the blue, and I felt very apprehensive about surgery, but on the other hand I quickly realised that I would be very foolish to pass up the opportunity. What was more, it didn't give me a chance to sit around thinking about it for weeks. I said yes and he admitted that he had brought the nurse with him to help him convince me it was a good idea – they didn't need to!

As soon as they left to make the preparations, I got the phone and called William on his mobile, "Where are you?" I asked. "Well, actually I'm in a shop buying a mop for the kitchen floor, I have to have the place nice for you coming home today, you know!" "Forget the kitchen floor!" I said, "I'm going into surgery in a few hours!" The mop stayed in the shop, and a couple of hours later he was by my side. We were able to talk together for a while and he re-assured me that I was in good hands with my consultant and his surgical team; after all, surely this was the type of operation that they had performed thousands of times before?

At that point in time we both certainly had faith in God and committed the situation to Him in prayer, but I have to admit that my ultimate trust was in the medical staff and, in particular, in my consultant surgeon. I was brought down to the theatre and felt very nervous indeed, until I saw the familiar face that was Aidan. "I'm very much hoping that we will be able to save the kidney as planned," he said, "but if there is a life-threatening clot, it may have to go."

He gave me a reassuring smile and went off to scrub up, and I was asked to sign a form before the anaesthetist came to see me. At this point my thoughts were going wild, the words "life–threatening" were echoing in my head. It was only then that it struck me how serious this operation actually was. If anything should go wrong I might not see my little girl, my husband, my family again.

They were preparing me for surgery and trying to get a line into my arm, and the tears began rolling down my cheeks. The nurse apologised, thinking they had hurt me with the needle, but the tears that flowed were coming from a much deeper hurt than that. Soon the anaesthetic kicked in and I slipped from consciousness.

About five hours later I woke up in the recovery room surrounded by monitors flashing and beeping. My first thoughts were, "Oh, oh oh, I'm in a lot of pain, but at least that means I must be alive!" Aidan came into the recovery room and said that he was pleased that the operation had gone well and the tumour was all away. It was quite a relief to hear that news, even through the pain that I was in. Now it was just going to be a question of how long it would take me to recover; and surely the worst was over, at least that's what I liked to think.

So it was that my expected 3 days in hospital stretched to over 3 weeks. During this time the children were settling into school, and William was doing his best to juggle family, work, and visits to the hospital. At least one of the things he didn't have to worry about was cooking. The Newcastle folks brought meals to the door almost every day. The boys thought that this was great! One of their firm favourites was numerous varieties of chicken and broccoli bake - they called it Methodist Pie and it went down a treat with them!

At this time Andy was due to go back to school in Dungannon, and William said, "What am I going to do with Olivia now?" Andy said, "Do you remember that man on Sunday, who said if you need any help, just let us know – well, why don't we let him know?"

William contacted Malcolm and Liz McKeown who, although being members of our Dundrum congregation, lived just around the corner from our manse in Newcastle. They happily agreed to collect Olivia from school and look after her any time that William needed to be at the hospital with me. Olivia became very close to them and treated their home as her home.

I was glad to hear that the children were being so well looked after, but I was anxious to get home as soon as the results of the tests being carried out had come through. I was very hopeful that these lab tests would prove that the tumour was benign, and life could get back to normal after I recovered from surgery. However, things did not work out that way at all.

The first thing that happened was that I was told the lab tests would not be back before my discharge day, and we would have to return to the hospital for the results after a couple of weeks, which we did. Mr O'Brien was away in the States by this time, so it fell to one of his team to tell us that the tests in Craigavon had proved to be inconclusive, and therefore they had sent biopsies over to London and Glasgow in order for them to give an opinion on the nature of the tumour. It meant a further wait, but at this stage I remained hopeful that it was just standard procedure and tried not to let my thoughts, and especially my fears, get the better of me.

A few more weeks went by until we heard that the responses from both London and Glasgow were also inconclusive, which was a worrying development. In a further meeting, we were told that the tumour had turned out to be extremely rare. In fact, on a scale of one to ten, if 'one' is commonplace, then the tumour which has been removed would be considered to be at 'ten' for rarity.

The decision had, therefore, been made to send the biopsy to Harvard University Hospital in Boston for further investigation and analysis, the results of which would take about two months. It seemed like a long time, but we were still hopeful that the results would eventually turn out to be clear.

One evening, towards the end of November, we received the news that we didn't want to hear. I had fancied a change of colour in the living room in time for Christmas, and William was up a stepladder wallpapering, when the telephone rang. I was surprised to hear my consultant on the end of the phone and then William saw the look of surprise turn to shock as he told me why he had called. The report had come back from Harvard, and the tumour had proved to contain malignant cancer cells. The conclusions they reached were supported by the other investigations, so there could be no doubt about their results. On the other hand, there was still real cause for optimism that all of the cancer had come away when the tumour had been removed, and if that was the case, things would turn out alright.

The bottom line was that because of the nature of the cells involved, and in response to these results, Harvard had made the recommendation that I should be scanned every three months in order to ensure that there was no further recurrence. Now I was facing regular kidney scans for the foreseeable future beginning at the end of January 2004. We sat down and considered the situation before us, trying to consider the best and worst case scenarios

It seemed to us that at best the scans would show that the cancer was all away, but that even in the event of this not being so, the worst case was the option of a kidney being removed. I didn't really want to consider this option too much as I was still slowly recovering from my previous surgery, but at least we knew that the cancer would be isolated then, and as I had found out before my original surgery, the removal of one kidney would not be the end of the world.

We all did our best to put it to the back of our minds as we entered into the Christmas spirit and all the carol services, visits and gifts that surround a circuit of three churches at that time of year. We love to sing carols, but this year even they seemed to have a freshness about them, such as "Hark the Herald Angels Sing ..."

"Light and life to all he brings,
Risen with healing in his wings ..."

We heard such very familiar words in a new way as we certainly needed that light in the dark days, and that life to keep us going, but we were as yet unaware what the resurrection healing power of Jesus was really about.

When all the work was done, and three early morning services were completed, we were able to close the manse door and enjoy Christmas Day with the family. Over the years we have developed our own tradition whereby the children would open one small gift before church to bring with them, one when they got home, and the main ones as we all sat around the Christmas tree.

This was done after dinner when all had been tidied away in the kitchen, so that everyone could enjoy the occasion. It was a really lovely time together with Olivia doing her little 'job' of checking the names on the labels, and passing out the presents which were gathered under the tree.

At times, it was difficult enough to concentrate on the festivities with all the medical information in the background, but at least we knew that the scan in January would settle things and we could get back to some degree of normality again – surely the New Year of 2004 would bring some good news? We could only wait and see ...

8

'CHANCE' ENCOUNTERS

My scan took place towards the end of January, and in February we were preparing to go to Donegal for a special extra Methodist Minister's Conference called Re:Call. All ministers were required to go, and I hadn't really wanted to be on my own for a week, so we had made arrangements to stay with our friends Stewart and Shirley who had just built a beautiful house in Loughros Point in Ardara, a few miles from the conference location. Stewart was the Methodist minister whom we had known so well from our early days in Bray Methodist Church, and they planned to travel together each day.

The keynote speaker at the conference was Paul Reid, the pastor of Christian Fellowship Church in Belfast, and an excellent communicator. William was looking forward to hearing him addressing his chosen topic, the title of which he took from a book that was out at the time, "If you want to walk on water – you've got to get out of the boat".

I was looking forward to a nice break, and hadn't expected to hear about my test results until I came back, but then the telephone rang. I had a definite sense of déjà vu, as I heard Aidan O'Brien's voice on the line once again. He said that my results had just come through, and he would have brought us into his office to tell us about them, but he knew we were going away to Donegal, the following day, and he felt we should be aware of them. There wasn't any easy way to tell me that they weren't clear as we had been hoping for, instead they had shown up lesions on my kidneys again, where the tumour had been removed.

I would have to go back into hospital after three months for more scanning. Further radical surgery and the potential removal of a kidney was a definite option, so we could still rely on a medical solution to the problem – at least that's what we thought! It was not the news we expected or wanted to hear, and we set off for Donegal in a sombre mood. As we drove, William put on a CD with worship led by Robin Mark, the worship leader at CFC, where Paul is the pastor. The words of one particular song really ministered to me, bringing a sense of peace to the turmoil I was feeling in my heart.

No not by might,
nor even power,
but by Your Spirit, O Lord.
Healer of hearts,
Binder of wounds,
Lives that are lost, restore
Flow through this land,
Till every man
Praises Your name
once more.

© Robin Mark

At the very beginning of the conference, the participants were asked to turn to the person next to them, and say why they had come, and what their expectations were. William found himself standing beside Mairisine Stanfield, a Presbyterian minister who was a guest speaker at some of the seminars. She didn't know anything about our situation and when she asked William why he had come, he said very honestly, "Quite frankly, I'm here because I was told that I had to be here, although my mind isn't really on the conference at all. I do hope I hear something helpful." With the news that we had just heard, he would rather have been at home with me.

That brief conversation wasn't the only one they had. The next time there was a short break in the proceedings, Mairisine walked straight over to William and said, "I feel that I need to encourage you with a picture the Lord has put in my mind." Although somewhat bemused by this, William listened carefully, for he could do with some encouragement. "This is not for now, but for the future," she said. Then she asked a most peculiar question, "Have you ever seen the movie Braveheart?" William said that he had, in fact, it was one of his favourites. He supposed it was something to do with having some Scottish blood a few generations back – he thought to himself, "this girl's Scottish – I can see why she would like it!"

Mairisine continued, "You remember the time when Mel Gibson rides up and down in front of the clans, and they're all standing there looking quite afraid and hesitant in the face of the battle against what seems to be overwhelming odds?" "Oh yes, that's got to be the best part of the movie," replied William. "Well," she said, "the picture that I have for you from the Lord is that I could see you doing exactly that for the Body of Christ. He's calling you to ride up and down, not in your own strength, but in the power of the Holy Spirit, proclaiming freedom from fear, giving hope to His people, encouraging them to claim the victory, even when it all looks lost, for the battle is the Lord's!"

"That's quite a picture," said William, "I sure don't feel like that at the moment." "Hold on to it," she said, "when the time is right, you'll see it too." That was one of a number of "chance encounters" we were to have over the coming months, which we later recognised as the Lord's hand on our lives. Later on, as William shared with me about the "battle picture" that he had been given, the words of Robin's song, taken from Scripture, came back into my mind.

"No not by might,
nor even power,
but by Your Spirit, O Lord."

Paul had spoken really well and used his theme to encourage the folks attending to step out of their "comfort zone" and rely completely on the leading of the Holy Spirit in their lives. As we travelled home from the conference, we had little idea of just how far outside that comfort zone we would find ourselves in the coming days.

During this time it was good to know that so many people were praying for us, especially the folks in our own church. We also got to know Steven and Donna. Well, actually, Steven and William met first, in a rather bizarre way! Steven was the pastor of the Elim Pentecostal church in Newcastle, and they had both arrived one morning to lead the assembly at Olivia's school, Newcastle Primary, to date neither has admitted to being the one who turned up on the wrong day!

When the principal asked which one of them would like to stay and take the assembly, William mentioned that he would be happy to do it the following week instead as he was rushing away immediately afterwards to bring me to a hospital appointment. Steven asked what was happening, and when he heard the latest news, he promised that he and the folks in his church would keep us in prayer. They agreed to meet for coffee sometime, and left it at that. God has His own ways of arranging events for a purpose – we had no idea at that time just how that "chance" meeting would result in a strong and lasting friendship which would last through many good days ... and bad.

9

THE SILVER TEATRAY

The day came at the end of April when I was to be admitted to hospital. It was a pleasant enough room, and I could see the Mountains of Mourne quite clearly in the distance, and I just wished that I could be back with the family in our manse which was a stone's throw from them. The weather had been beautiful in that week coming up to the Bank holiday weekend, and it would have suited me very well to be there, instead of in a hospital bed.

A few days went by, and I was in and out of the room regularly for various further procedures and scanning, and endless blood tests. I thought about the long and painful road that I had been down since the first time I had been told that I would need surgery. It had been a much bigger operation than I had anticipated at the time. For the first few weeks after surgery, even a sneeze or a cough seemed to radiate pain through my body. Over time it had begun to ease, I started to get out and about walking for a short time at first, and gradually increasing the distances as my body started to heal up. By now I was able to manage very well, taking walks around the parks and along the prom in Newcastle. The idea of going right back to where I was at the start was not something I wanted to contemplate at all.

During this spell in hospital, however, I had come to accept the idea that if it was going to take further surgery to sort out the problem, then so be it. However, I was also still hoping that my scans would reveal better news, but it was not to be.

On Friday evening, the 30th of April, another date that I will never forget, William and I were waiting for some news when at about 6.30, Aidan came into the room, carrying a file. Before he opened his mouth, I could tell by the look on his face that things were not as good as we all had hoped for. He sat on the end of the bed and first told us that he had taken the decision not to remove my kidney at this point. William and I looked at each other and breathed a huge sigh of relief. I had definitely not been looking forward to another operation, and this was the news I had been longing to hear – but why did Aidan have that look on his face? Surely this was good news?

He was silent for a moment, drew breath, and said, "That is the good news, but I'm afraid that the bad news is that lesions have now appeared on your lungs." When he said this, the enormity of it didn't really sink in. I remember thinking that this would probably mean that I would be transferred to a department other than Urology, which might mean having to see a different consultant.

I wanted to know what happened next, as in what treatment or surgery I would need. Again there was a long pause and a deep breath. His response was devastating, "If it turns out to be secondaries on the lungs, then it will lead to your death."

I couldn't believe what I was hearing, neither could William. It was all a blur. He kept on talking but by then I wasn't really listening. I felt so frightened and upset and I was shaking uncontrollably.

Aidan went on to say I was to be referred to a specialist cancer consultant in Belfast's Belvoir Park hospital, and after a few more comments he left the room. A nurse stayed and tried to console me, saying that I would come to terms with the news, and asking about my children. I'm sure she was doing her best in a very difficult situation, but the idea of coming to terms with what I had just been told was a million miles away from my mind at that moment in time.

It was the strangest feeling – for just a moment after he had said I wouldn't be having the kidney operation it had seemed that things were looking up, I wouldn't have to face that pain, that recovery time all over again, just a few seconds later, it seemed that my whole world had collapsed in ruins. It all seemed surreal, as if everything was now moving in slow motion. We were both in total shock.

In the middle of it all a peculiar thing happened. The door opened and a nurse came in carrying a silver teatray complete with silver teapot, china cups, napkins, and chocolate biscuits! She set it down on a table without saying a word and left just as quickly as she had arrived. It's amazing what goes through your mind in a situation like this. William looked at it sitting there on the table and thought, "I've only ever seen wooden trays and stainless steel teapots in this place – certainly never chocolate biscuits ... things must REALLY be bad!" It almost felt like a condemned person's last meal, and it seemed to add to that whole surreal feeling surrounding the news that we had just been given.

I was still shaking and crying, and the nurse said that she would ask Mr O'Brien to come back in to speak further with us. We wanted to have some hope, some way out of this. We wanted to turn the clock back and undo the words that he had said, but it was not to be.

Just then my mobile phone rang. It was my sister, calling from Dublin to see how I had got on with my results. As I told her through the sobbing what had happened we both just cried together over the telephone line. She tried to find some words of consolation but my heart was breaking. I knew that she couldn't quite believe the words that she was hearing, I couldn't believe them either. Still, it was lovely to hear her voice at the end of the phone. I could only imagine how she felt when we finished that brief conversation.

After a short while Aidan came back into the room and William asked if there was any treatment at all that would help. At that point he said that there was always treatment, but that with the prognosis we had been given the result would ultimately be the same as he had spelled out earlier. We talked for a little while longer and he explained that he had always been honest with us and would continue to be all along the way. He had struggled with having to break this news but in the end, if we were to continue to have confidence in him, there was no point holding back.

Whether good news or bad news, we knew that we could trust him in whatever he said ... unfortunately, it had all been bad news so far, and it wasn't showing signs of getting any better. I had been due to be discharged on Saturday, but I just wanted to get out of the hospital as fast as I could and Aidan said that it would be fine, just as soon as he signed the usual letters.

The door closed and for the first time we were left alone in the room. I got dressed, quickly shoving all my things into a bag, but I was in a state of shock. It was all too much for me. Every TV programme I had ever seen, every magazine article I had ever read, every story I had ever heard about what cancer and cancer treatment can do flooded through my mind. I turned and hammered with my fists against the glass in the windows that ran the full length of my room. I'm sure at the time that I didn't care if they had shattered, such was my despair. William pulled me away from the window and put his strong arms around me as I sobbed into his chest soaking his shirt with my tears. "Don't worry, love," he said, "we'll get through this together ... there has to be a way, there has to be ..."

10

THROUGH THE VALLEY

We took the long drive home to Newcastle and it was a beautiful Friday evening, the beginning of the May Bank Holiday weekend. There were lots of cars on the road heading for Newcastle, and as we drew closer, I noticed how beautiful the Mournes were looking as the evening sun cast its glimmers of light over the tops of the mountains and the shadows began to lengthen in the valleys between them. William had noticed them too, and the words of Psalm 23 came into his mind ...

"Yea though I walk through the valley
of the shadow of death, I will fear no evil."

But I did fear at that time, I feared a great deal. I feared for my family, I feared for my husband, and I feared for myself. In the valley of the shadow I had found not peace, but hopelessness and despair. Maybe that was the moment when I started to realise that I had ultimately put most of my hope and trust in hospitals, consultants, and medical procedures. Of course, I had prayed, and I knew others had been praying for me, but where was all that now when it really mattered, when it hurt so much? In the harsh light of the reality of my prognosis, I was facing the greatest challenge of my life, and I wasn't sure where to start.

I knew that I believed in heaven, I knew as a born-again Christian that I was going to be there with the Lord someday. But 'someday' always seemed so far away. Now I was staring death in the face, and as a mum with a young family I felt as if I just wasn't ready for that. Desperately I tried to find hope from somewhere within, but, as I would learn in the coming days and weeks, if it's not inside it can't come out. I didn't know how to apply the healing verses of scripture. I didn't even know where most of them were. I certainly had a degree of faith, but the Word of faith, that Word that is life giving and life sustaining had not been established deep in my life and in my heart. I just felt empty and numb. I would never forget that feeling, and I'm determined never to feel it again.

We arrived in Newcastle and decided to call to see Malcolm and Liz, who had become close friends over those weeks. They had been so good to us, looking after Olivia when we had hospital appointments, and making meals for the boys. Their home had been like an oasis, somewhere we could call day or night, and have good coffee and a chat, but now we had to break the news they had never expected to hear. As we shared what had happened they just held me close as I cried. They didn't say much, they didn't need to. They just listened as I poured out my heart. We knew they really cared, and that was all that mattered at the time.

When we eventually arrived home, we had to break the news to my mother who was staying with us for a few days. That was a really difficult thing to do. As I picked up a picture of Olivia and hugged it close to me, my heart felt as if it was breaking in two. Among the many things that went through my mind was the fact that my Grandmother on my dad's side was in her ninety-ninth year when she died. "I haven't even lived half of the length of her life," I thought.

I went to bed but I never slept at all – not for one minute. I just cried all night long as I tried to come to terms with all that I had heard. William has often said since that he didn't realise up to then that it was physically possible to cry so many tears for such a long time. While comforting me, he spent time in prayer, crying out to the Lord in a more intense way than he had ever done before.

When dawn broke, he turned to me and said, "I really believe that it's not your time, you are going to live – we are going to claim life for you – and we're going to see what the Word of God has to say about this." I didn't feel that way at that time. I didn't feel anything, just a sense of numbness. I looked at a daily reading by Kay Arthur which began with the words, *"Do not fear! – Moment by moment the Lord will see you through each day if you live by faith."* Combined with William's words, it was the encouragement I needed to start seeking that word for myself, but it was to be a long walk through many more tears.

I knew that I didn't want to have another sleepless might so I rang the doctor on call. She agreed to send a prescription for sleeping tablets to our local chemist, with the warning that they were potentially addictive and therefore only to be treated as a short term solution. It was a beautiful Saturday afternoon on the May Bank Holiday weekend, and we left Olivia with my mum and headed for the town, which took us past Malcolm and Liz's house. William stopped off to chat with Malcolm while Liz said she would walk with me to the chemist. We strolled down through the park by the river, the sun glistening on the water, the mountains clearly defined against a cloudless sky. As we came to the mouth of the river, near where it flowed down to the sea Liz showed me the new family of ducklings which she had shown to Olivia a few days before. There I saw new vibrant life reminding me of the fragility of my own.

As we emerged onto the promenade just beside the pharmacy, I could see that the beach was packed with families enjoying the Bank Holiday sand, sea, and sun. I experienced for the first time what it feels like to have the world spinning around me, carrying on with life as usual, while I felt like mine had stopped. I wanted to scream, "Stop! Don't you know what's happening to me?" My emotions really were all over the place. Liz could see that I was upset and asked if I was okay. I could only express how I felt by saying, "Liz, the sun shouldn't be shining today." She comforted me with the words,"Sharyn, none of us know what tomorrow may bring, just enjoy each day the Lord has given to us." She was right, of course, somehow I had to see past my circumstances and hear what the Lord was saying in all this, and the only place that I would find that was in His Word.

That evening we sat down and prayed together, and William gave me a small red book to record my feelings and any verses that the Lord gave us during this time. It was a very personal thing for me, and I certainly never expected anyone else to read it! I had found one verse that very day which had immediately ministered to me. So I wrote across the top of the first page of my journal

> *"1st May 2004 - By his stripes, I am healed*
> *– My Story of how God healed me."*

We started to search the Scriptures to see what they had to say about God's healing power. As we talked and read together, we began to realise that somewhere along the way we had both picked up on the idea that God sometimes "gave" sickness to people in order to help them get closer to him, or teach them some sort of a lesson in life.

Many times we had heard people describe this with phrases such as "this is my cross to bear". So it was that the first thing we had to come to terms with was the question, "Did God give me my cancer, for whatever reason?" It seemed to us that if He did, then there wasn't much point praying for healing, because that would be going against His will for my life, and therefore I would miss out on whatever the lesson was that I was supposed to learn. There may be many different reasons and circumstances that result is such a disease being present in a person's body, but at that time it was the only question to which I wanted an answer, because that answer would determine how I would react to it.

On the other hand, if God did not give me my cancer, then it wasn't 'MY' cancer at all. It was in my body illegally, and I could and should not accept it, but instead do anything and everything I could to beat it. My pattern for approaching it had to be the Saviour's pattern. So what did Jesus do when confronted by sickness in his earthly ministry, and what did the people do who encountered him?

I read about the woman in Mark chapter 5 who had been ill for such a long time, and used every medical avenue available to her, but to no avail. Yet she did not give in to her sickness, instead she waited for her moment, and pressed through the crowd, just to touch the hem of Jesus' garment, using every ounce of faith that she possessed. Of course, this was a story I had known since Sunday School days, but now I could see her pain and feel her determination to beat this thing that had ruined her life up to that moment as she reached out to the Master. I could no longer see her as a character in a Bible story, but a totally real person just like me, who had struggled with the same emotions and fears that I was now feeling. She would have simply melted back into the crowd, but Jesus wanted to know who had touched him – he knew healing virtue had flowed out of him …

"Then the woman, seeing that she could not go unnoticed, came trembling and fell at his feet. In the presence of all the people, she told why she had touched him and how she had been instantly healed."

Unlike those who were surrounding her, and tried to keep her away from Jesus, He did not despise her faith in His healing power, instead His response to her was to say,

"Daughter, be of good comfort, your faith has made you whole, go in peace."

I reached a very simple conclusion. If faith in Jesus' healing power was the key to that woman's healing, then it would prove to be the key to my healing also. I determined that I too would press through the crowd, whatever it took, even if people told me not to bother the Master, and just accept things as they were. I wanted to know the same comfort, peace, and healing virtue that had made that woman whole, flowing into my own life.

I was walking through the valley of the shadow, but I was beginning to believe that that it was THROUGH the valley I would go. I had no intention of lying down in it just yet.

11

NEW LIFE - NEW FIGHT

I continued to keep my journal, recording the feelings and emotions that I had and the way in which the Lord spoke to me as I started to claim the healing verses from His Word every day. In many ways I began to see it like medicine for my ailing body, as it says in Proverbs 4: 20-22,

20 *"... give attention to my words;*
     Incline your ear to my sayings.
21 *Do not let them depart from your sight;*
     Keep them in the midst of your heart.
22 *For they are life to those who find them*
     And health to all their body."

As I kept the words of Scripture in front of my eyes and in my heart, I knew that they would bring life and health to me, building up my faith little by little, making it stronger and stronger. I was prepared to go anywhere and do anything that it would take as long as it brought me closer to the Lord. Christian media too played an important role in all of this. For years I had tended to watch Coronation Street, Eastenders, Emmerdale and lots of other soaps and TV programmes. Suddenly, as we flicked through the satellite menu we discovered Christian TV, and started to tune in regularly to TBN, The God Channel, Revelation, and since then Loveworld, Daystar and Inspiration Network. It was all part of the process of soaking in the Word, and being open to many different ways that God was using to speak into my life.

One Thursday evening we happened to tune into UCB Radio and they were broadcasting live from the NEC in Birmingham, where the Joyce Meyer Ministries conference was taking place. We had only ever heard her very occasionally on the radio, but we were amazed when the first thing that she said was that she had done something she rarely did in her ministry. She had completely changed the series of planned talks and now would be speaking on the subject of "Overcoming Fear". The talks were so tuned in to my situation that although there were thousands attending the conference, it felt as if they had been changed just for me! The main verse that stayed with me was 1 John 4:18,

> *"there is no fear in love,*
> *for perfect love casts out all fear."*

I realised that if I wanted to beat the fear that was gripping my heart, then I would have to find the solution in the perfect love that comes from Jesus alone, but I also realised that it was going to be a real battle to get to that place. Together, William and I would fight that battle. After all, it was a battle for my life. It then took us a while to understand that the battle was not ours, but the Lord's. The victory had already been won 2,000 years ago. That understanding would come in time, as I learned to stop wrestling, and start resting, in Him.

Both of our families were a great encouragement at that time. My brother Rodney told his office staff that if I called I was to be put straight through to him. I have often thought that it must have been especially difficult for him as he had been through the experience of losing his best friend Reggie to illness a few years before. Both he and my sister would talk to me any time day or night. William's sister Vie would be happy to talk to me until 3am assuring me of the Lord's love for me in my situation.

Shortly after receiving my news, Norma suggested that it might help to talk to my cousin Joan, who had cancer over a number of years. Joan and Billy lived in Dublin, but they didn't hesitate to agree to meet with us. They drove up to a hotel near Newry where they treated us to a lovely lunch. She was really helpful, and also showed me much love. I knew that she understood what I was going through and that the Lord would be with me through these hard days. We will always be so thankful for Billy and Joan's encouragement when I needed it most.

The following Saturday was the 8th of May, and that day, in the midst of all my heartache and pain, we had a phone call from Kelvin to say that our first Grandson had been born at 9.30am. We were at Steven and Donna's home that day, and we spent some time praying together before we travelled over to see him. As Donna laid hands on me I felt a heat going through my body and an incredible sense of peace washed over me.

I really did need that peace as baby William had been born in the very same hospital where I had been given my bad news, and I hadn't been back there since. A shiver went down my spine as we parked and I glanced up at the window of the room I had been in that evening. As I walked through the hospital corridors towards the maternity unit, all the words I had heard just eight days before flooded back into my mind. It was a day of very mixed emotions for me. I was delighted that the baby had arrived safe and well, but as I held him in my arms I wondered if I would even live to see his first birthday.

It wasn't very likely if the news I had been given came to pass, but as I held this brand new life in my arms I set my mind to claiming every promise about healing that I could find in the Word, determined to claim back my life from the words of death that had been spoken over me. This new life that I held in my arms gave me new hope for the future, and I had every intention of sharing it with my family. I was going to fight this thing that was threatening to kill me, and with God's help, I was going to win.

One evening we were watching a live programme on the God Channel called "A Call to Prayer" hosted by Rory and Wendy Alec. They had on as special guests Pastor Roy Harthern and his wife Pauline, now based in Stoke-on-Trent. They shared how he had been in hospital and told there was no hope because of advanced kidney cancer. Pauline told how she simply wouldn't accept this and stood in the hospital room rebuking the cancer in her husband's body in the name of Jesus. He recovered completely, and scans later revealed that he had miraculously been given a brand new set of kidneys without any surgery. William turned to me and said, "If that lady could believe God's healing power for her husband, then I can surely believe it for my wife!"

We started to agree together for my healing no matter what medical reports might come our way or how bad they might be; our resolve to do this would be tested to the very limit. (We have met with Roy and Pauline a couple of times since then, and I'm pleased to say that he is still as healthy as ever!)

While hearing testimonies like this were really helpful to building faith, the main source was the Word itself, and reading through the Psalms continued to assure me that emotions of despair and even anger were there, as well as love, joy and peace. I realised that the psalmists were real people, writing not just pretty words, but real words describing real lives, much like I was doing as I kept my journal. I had never expected anyone to read it, or extracts from it, I just knew that I would never want to forget how I felt as I went through those dark days, which now and again saw rays of light breaking through the clouds of despair.

One such ray of light came in the words of Psalm 103:1-3,

1 *"Praise the Lord, O my soul;*
   all my inmost being, praise his holy name.
2 *Praise the Lord, O my soul,*
   and forget not all his benefits -
3 *who forgives all your sins*
   and heals all your diseases."

These were such powerful words to me, helping me to realise that healing begins with worship and praise, putting the Lord in his rightful place in our lives. William sometimes shares about the time that we checked into a hotel in London and were given a keycard which let us into the room. As we settled in we noticed a folder lying on the dressing table which invited us to read it "to gain maximum enjoyment from your stay with us". We left it lying there and went down to dinner.

Later on, however, William picked it up and began to read through it. It turned out that the keycard not only allowed us into the room, but also admitted us to the club lounge, a very plush area in which we could have breakfast, access the internet, and enjoy all the facilities available. If we hadn't read the folder, or simply chosen to ignore it, we would never have known that there were a lot more benefits to having that key, than simply getting into our room.

As we read Psalm 103, we realised that the principle was just the same. Here was the truth we had failed to really appreciate – if we were going to prevail in this battle against sickness, then we had to grasp the fact that the same Lord who had made provision to forgive my sin, had also made provision to heal my disease.

The lesson of the unread hotel folder applies just as much to the Word of God. We need to become aware of "ALL the benefits" that He has made available to us as His children. If only we would read about them in the folder He has given to us – His precious Word, we would be able to claim them for ourselves.

12

NINETY-ONE

Life was going on around us during this time, and I tried my best to continue to do the normal things around the home, church and school. We had plans in place to begin a new coffee bar outreach in our Newcastle Church in the summer, which was well placed on the Central Promenade to attract young people who would be in town for the holidays and weekend breaks. So we began to get the different things needed to put it together, from tables to candle holders!

We also had plans in place for the new community-wide Alpha Course, which was to begin at the end of the summer, and preparations were well under way for that, including getting Alpha International to raise the profile by placing Alpha posters on all the buses during the holiday season.

It was all part of the process of walking in the belief that I was going to be well and not giving in to the prognosis I had been given. During each day different things happened to me –

some good, some bad. It was lovely to get cards and emails encouraging me, and sometimes having a coffee in the town, people I had never seen before would come along and say, "You don't know me, but I heard what happened, and I'm praying for you." That was really encouraging, if a little disconcerting at first!

At other times I would just burst into tears, such as on Olivia's Sports Day. As I watched her, she was smiling and singing as usual, and I thought about her growing up possibly without me. I began to think the same thing about the boys – would I see them complete school, go to University, take up their future careers?

One day when we were having some fellowship with Steven and Donna, he prayed that I would live to see Olivia married.

That evening I wrote in my journal,

"My hearts desire is to see her growing up, and be there for her in her childhood, to hug and kiss, and do girlie things together.
I want to be able to tell her how sick I was, and how the Lord healed her mummy."

Only someone who has been given the sort of news that I heard, and was to hear, can really understand the trauma that you go through emotionally when words like that are spoken over you, no matter how strong or weak a man or woman of faith you may be.

When I was a young girl in school, we used to rhyme at the boys across the playground,

"Sticks and stones will break my bones,
but words will never harm me!"

How untrue that is! I have learned that words, those that we speak out in our own lives, those that we speak into others, and words that are spoken over us, can have a huge effect on us.

Sometimes I just didn't want to come out of the house because some well-meaning person might say something that would send me spiralling downwards into negativity and despair.

Night-time tended to be the worst, when everyone else was asleep in the house, and in my mind I would re-live again and again the words that I had heard in the hospital, and elsewhere, and I would wake up gripped by fear. However, when I eventually brought myself to focus on the love that the Lord has for me, that fear would go. Paul wrote in his letter to the Romans,

> *"The Word is near you; it is in your mouth and in your heart.*
> *That is, the Word of faith we are proclaiming to you."*
> (Romans 10:8-9)

We were learning each day that the way to come against these things was to apply the Word of God by faith, even in the midst of fear, despite the roller-coaster of emotions I felt that I was riding most days.

During this time William and I were even closer than we had ever been before in our relationship. When I found it hard to sleep, he would light some candles in the room and lie beside me, stroking my hair and whispering words of love and encouragement to me until I drifted off to sleep.

A number of times, when we were at our closest together, I would burst into tears at the thought of our being parted from each other. I just couldn't help it, we loved each other so much.

One day when we were reading together we came across Psalm 91; even though I had read many healing verses this seemed to really touch me very deeply, and would prove to be for me the answer to those words of discouragement which had been pulling me down.

Psalm 91

1 *She who dwells in the shelter of the Most High*
   will rest in the shadow of the Almighty.
2 *I will say of the LORD, "He is my refuge and my*
   fortress, my God, in whom I trust."
3 *Surely he will save you from the fowler's snare*
   and from the deadly pestilence.
4 *He will cover you with his feathers,*
   and under his wings you will find refuge;
   his faithfulness will be your shield and rampart.
5 *You will not fear the terror of night,*
   nor the arrow that flies by day,
6 *nor the pestilence that stalks in the darkness,*
   nor the plague that destroys at midday.
7 *A thousand may fall at your side,*
   ten thousand at your right hand,
   but it will not come near you.
8 *You will only observe with your eyes*
   and see the punishment of the wicked.
9 *If you make the Most High your dwelling -*
   even the LORD, who is my refuge -
10 *then no harm will befall you,*
   no disaster will come near your tent.
11 *For he will command his angels concerning you*
   to guard you in all your ways.

Whenever disaster strikes, or an emergency comes in mycountry, we reach for the telephone and dial 999, but in the USA there is a different number to dial – 911. As I looked at the first verse of this psalm I realised that it could be my 'emergency line' – Psalm 91 verse 1 was a place where I could learn to dwell in the shelter of the Most High; I would exchange the shadow of death for the shadow of the Almighty. He would cover me with his feathers, and under his wings I would find refuge.

Later in the Psalm were more words that spoke straight to my heart –

"you will not fear the terror of night."

I read the Psalm every morning and every night, taking the words like medicine into me, as surely as I would take a doctor's prescription. If I woke up during the night I would claim those words, rebuke that fear and terror, receive a real sense of peace and go back to sleep again.

I didn't need the sleeping tablets any more, so I stopped taking them. Resting in His peace was better than anything pills could provide. This Psalm would sustain me over the coming weeks and months, and is still one that I read every day even now.

I was calling on the Lord and knew He was with me in trouble, but I also wanted to be delivered, and I was certainly claiming long life.

14 *"Because she loves me," says the LORD, "I will rescue her;*
    I will protect her, for she acknowledges my name.
15 *She will call upon me, and I will answer her;*
    I will be with her in trouble,
    I will deliver her and honour her.
16 *With long life will I satisfy her*
    and show her my salvation."

13

THE VOICE OF HOPE

As we continued to discover during all of these experiences – God has a way of turning even small problems around. I was scheduled to have my main MRI scan in Belvoir Park cancer hospital on Thursday the 17th of June. I had to be at the Belfast hospital at 8am, which meant a very early start from Newcastle, but on the evening before I was due to go, something went wrong with the car that we had at that time, and despite William's best efforts, there was just no way to get it fixed in time. He rang Steven to ask him if he happened to know anybody who might be able to lend us a car at such short notice, but unknown to us Donna had a car also. She came to the rescue, and said that she would be happy for us to use it. Steven picked up William and brought him to his house to collect it so that he would be ready to take me to the hospital in the morning. It was great that we had the car problem solved so quickly, but God had more in store for us than simply a loan of a car.

During these days, music had played a huge part in keeping us grounded in the Word of God, as we walked daily by faith. Listening to CDs at home and in the car kept us in an atmosphere of praise and worship and helped us to stay focused on the Lord even when the circumstances surrounding us all combined to get us to take our eyes off Him. Donna said that she had only just returned from the "Cherish" Women's Conference at the Abundant Life Church in Bradford, and had left the CD "God is Here" in the car's CD player for us to listen to on the way to my appointment. "Make sure that Sharyn listens to that CD," she said, as she handed over the keys to William in their driveway, "I've left it ready on a particular track that I feel she should hear."

The next morning, as we drove to the hospital, we heard for the very first time the song that was to be a source of strength, hope and healing to us through the many dark days ahead. Written and sung by Abundant Life's Worship Pastor Lara Martin, we played "The Voice of Hope" over and over again as we made our way to one of my most difficult appointments so far. We had driven past the large metal gates of Belvoir Park Hospital many times, over the years, well known for their expertise in treating all kinds of cancer. I had often thought to myself that going through those gates must be one of the hardest things that anyone has to do. I had never imagined that I would be passing through them myself one day – but this was that day.

As we parked, I began to shake, wondering what this scan would reveal. We had left in good time and therefore had a few minutes to spare, so we prayed together, and rebuked my fear in the Name of Jesus. We held hands and closed our eyes in the midst of the storm as we let the music flood over us one more time before going through the doors of the hospital ...

"As high as the heavens are above the earth
So high are your ways to mine

Ways so perfect, they never fail me
I know you are good all the time!

And through the storm, Yet I will praise you
Despite it all, Yet I will sing
Through good or bad, Yet I will worship
For you remain the same King of Kings.

You are the Voice of Hope
The Anchor of my soul
Where there seems to be no way
You make it possible
You are the Prince of Peace
Amidst adversity
My lips will shout for joy
To you the Most High.

You were the One before time began
There's nothing beyond your control
My confidence, my assurance
Rest in your unchanging word!

And through the storm Yet I will praise you
Despite it all Yet I will sing
Through good or bad Yet I will worship
For you remain the same King of Kings

You are the Voice of Hope
The Anchor of my soul
Where there seems to be no way
You make it possible
You are the Prince of Peace
Amidst adversity
My lips will shout for joy
To you the Most High.

Lara Martin (Abundant Life Ministries, Wapping Road, Bradford, England.
From the CD/DVD "God is Here" www.alm.org.uk)© 2002 Thankyou Music/MCPS

The tears flowed as I placed myself afresh in the Lord's hands, trusting Him to make a way, even when there seemed to be none.

We have been in touch with Lara from time to time during the writing of this book, and were amazed to learn that she had written the song in the aftermath of 9/11, during her visit to Ground Zero in New York. She wrote to us telling us of her experience ...

Dear Sharyn and William,

I was on holiday in New York with my husband Jonathan shortly after 9/11. One day we went down to Ground Zero and I was amazed by the overwhelming amount of tributes that were hanging from railings, lampposts, trees, doorways etc. It was unbelievable. As I began to read some of them, I couldn't help but be overtaken with sadness. There were letters from children to their missing fathers, and messages from so many remembering their loved ones who had been taken from them.

At the time I remember thinking to myself, "Hope is missing. These people have no hope." There was a sound of fear about the future throughout most that I read.

Earlier that morning I had woken up with a melody running through my mind and right there at Ground Zero I began to piece a song together. It came with such ease. That song became 'The Voice of Hope'.

There is a scripture in Habakkuk 3:17-18 which also was inspirational to me at the time. It reads,

"Though the fig tree does not bud and there are no grapes on the vines,

though the olive crop fails and the fields produce no food, though there are no sheep in the pen and no cattle in the stalls, yet I will rejoice in the LORD, I will be joyful in God my Saviour."

This puts everything into perspective. It's easy to rejoice when things are going well but the true test is rejoicing in adversity. This is when it really costs and it truly becomes a sacrifice of praise. I believe this is what captures God's attention and draws a piece of heaven to earth. God can't help but get involved, it's in His nature.

I could never have imagined the impact this song would have on the lives of many that have heard or sang it. It has become a vehicle of healing to some and a literal voice of hope to those going through a storm ... He truly is the Voice of Hope to our lives.

When you know who God is you cannot help but look to the future with confidence despite your circumstances.

It's always a pleasure to hear from you.

God bless
Lara
January 2006

When we read this, we realised why the song had touched us so deeply, coming as it had out of a place of hopelessness. Now we were finding in God the hope to go on despite all the circumstances surrounding us.

Lara believes the impact of the song is in the fact that it is flooded with truth about who God is - His ways are higher than ours, His ways are perfect and unfailing, He's good all the time,

He was the one before time began, nothing is beyond His control, His Word is our assurance and confidence, He's the King of Kings, He's our shelter in the storm, He's the Prince of Peace.

With the song ringing in my ears, we got out of the car and I plucked up the courage to go into the scanning room, encouraged by some very attentive and helpful nursing staff. When it was all over, we drove home to await the results which, we expected, would come at my next appointment in a few weeks time. It occurred to me that through each new experience, I was learning day by day, as the song said, to put my confidence and assurance in His unchanging Word.

That is where my hope would be based in the coming days and weeks. Even through the times when hopelessness and despair seemed to be around every corner of life, He would be the Anchor of my Soul, and the Voice of Hope to my life.

14

BY HIS STRIPES

It seemed now that the only thing to do was get on with everyday life and wait for the call to come. I slept fairly well that night, and woke up on Friday morning aware that Olivia's 7th birthday was fast approaching on the 20th of June which was Sunday, and I set about making preparations for her special day. There was also a wedding to attend on Saturday which William was conducting and to which the Walker family had kindly invited myself and Olivia. It was quite unusual for her to be asked along to a wedding, so there was great excitement about this.

I had continued to keep my journal, writing down my thoughts and emotions every couple of days. The more I read what the Word of God said about healing, the more I felt faith rising up within me. One of the first verses I had read, I was now experiencing in my own life,

> *"Faith comes by hearing,*
> *and hearing by the Word of God."* (Romans 10:17)

Even when we are so beaten down by circumstances that we feel empty, lost and afraid, as we spend time in God's Word – faith COMES. Just a tiny mustard seed faith it may be, but Jesus said he can work with that if we allow Him to, even through the tears, and I had yet to shed many more of them.

William had gone out to a district church meeting in Lisburn, and I was in the house with Olivia at about 4 o'clock when the phone rang. Much to my surprise it was the appointments secretary from Belvoir Park Hospital. "Hello, is that Mrs Sharyn Mackay?" She wanted to be sure that she was giving the message to the right person. I was just sorry I'd answered the phone at all. I confirmed my identity and she continued, "We've had the results of your MRI scan yesterday and the Professor wants to see you as soon as possible."

I nearly dropped the telephone with the shock of this call. I know what the National Health Service is like, doing their very best with ever decreasing resources, and under pressure at the best of times. My next scheduled appointment was at the beginning of July, and if they wanted to see me this quickly, it could only be further bad news. Not only did they want to see me on Monday, but they had also referred me to one of their top cancer specialists, and he was going to fit me into another clinic which he held in Musgrave Park Hospital. As far as I could tell, they didn't even want to wait for one of his usual clinics in Belvoir Park.

It all seemed too much to take in. We had really good neighbours in Joe and Kitty, and she, another neighbour Mary, and Liz came and sat with me and made tea – the best Irish remedy for all adverse circumstances! It wasn't that long before William arrived home from his meeting, but it seemed like an age, and my voice was shaking so much he could hardly understand what I was saying.

I had so hoped that the scans would show some improvement to my condition, but if anything the urgency of my appointment could only suggest that things were now worse instead of better.

As the evening progressed my fear and despair seemed to turn to anger. It just welled up within me, it was all too much to take in. "Why was this happening to me? Why couldn't I get some good news for a change?" William walked through the door just as I took my journal, the place where I had been recording all my thoughts and words of faith, and tossed it onto the floor.

"So much for that," I said, as he picked it up, the red cover hanging off. "I suppose you and Steven will be changing your tune now about all these healing words you've been quoting!" Of course, it was just utter frustration as I had been quoting them just as much as they had!

William gently reminded me that the Psalms were full of frustration and heartache in difficult circumstances and so we sat and read some together.

I began to feel some sense of peace again, and after dinner we decided to go down to Steven and Donna's place for some fellowship and prayer. It's good to have friends who are prepared to stand with you in adversity, and stand with us they did. As we were leaving late that evening, Steven mentioned that there was a service on Sunday evening in their church that I should think about coming along to – a lady was speaking there who had a remarkable healing testimony. I thanked him for letting me know, but didn't really give it too much thought. I was determined to get through all that we had to do this weekend for Olivia's sake, but the appointment looming on Monday was always in the back of my mind.

On Saturday morning Olivia came into our room with great excitement. "It's the wedding day!" she said. I had arranged a hairdressing appointment for both of us, and she looked so beautiful with her hair all done, wearing the dress we had bought especially for the day. William was officiating and I was managing to hold myself together during the service until the second hymn "O Perfect Love". It was one of the hymns we had at our wedding on the 16th of May 1983 in Grosvenor Road Baptist Church in Dublin. It seemed like only yesterday and I could remember every detail of that day. Watching Heather about to take her vows, I could see myself standing next to William in my beautiful white wedding dress, so full of anticipation for a long and happy married life. Now it seemed like I was just being attacked with the thought that I wouldn't see many more anniversaries at all. "Lord, you're going to have to get me through this day," I prayed. "I'm believing your Word, I'm standing on your promises, but on a day like today, it's really, really hard. Thank you that you understand how I'm feeling."

As the day progressed it seemed like my thoughts moved from one extreme to the other, at times believing absolutely that I was going to be fine, but then drifting into thinking that at least the nice photographs that were being taken would be good for the family to have and remember me by, should the worst happen.

Apart from William, the only person who had an inkling of what I was going through was the bride's mother, Thelma. She was really sweet and kept checking to see if I was feeling okay, perhaps my face was displaying more of the turmoil inside than I had anticipated.

That evening when I got home I read the words again and again from 1 Peter 2:24,

> *"He himself bore our sins in his body on the tree, that we, being dead to sin, should live unto righteousness, by whose stripes we were healed."*

As I drifted off to sleep I repeated the words to myself, "By his stripes I was healed, By his stripes I was healed." It wasn't that Jesus had suddenly looked over the shoulder of the radiographer one day, noticed my scans and said, "Well, what am I going to do about this problem now?" No, He had done it 2,000 years ago on the cross, and what I needed to do was continue to claim it and believe that it was just as true for me today.

The Amplified Bible made this even clearer, as I feel it makes what Jesus did even more personal to each of us,

> *"He personally bore our sins in His [own] body on the tree, [as on an altar and offered Himself on it], that we might die (cease to exist) to sin and live to righteousness. By His wounds you have been healed."*

What powerful words they were for me at that time. I was trusting the Lord, and starting to learn what it was to really walk by faith, but emotionally that day was draining, and I expected that the next one would be much the same. I planned to just about get myself through Sunday while clinging on to those healing words – but God had other plans for me.

15

DIVINE APPOINTMENT

I woke up on Sunday morning feeling very low. Picking up my journal I wrote,

> *"Seven years ago today my little girl was born, I was so happy then, but now things feel so wrong, I'm so frightened of what tomorrow will bring when I go for my results."*

Whenever I started to feel like that, the only thing I could do was reach for my Bible, and hold on to some healing verses to get me through the day. The more we read and relied on God's Word, the more I was learning that I needed to believe, even before I could see.

> *"For we walk by faith and not by sight."*
> (2 Corinthians 5:7)

We had sent out an email a few days before to encourage friends to pray. Part of it read - *"We are trusting that the Lord will heal me, and that He, and not the doctors hold the words for my life."*

We went to church where William was preaching about prayer that morning, and I could tell that it really came from the heart. He reminded the congregation of something he had mentioned a few weeks before and held up a sheet with the word "PUSH" printed on it. This stands for "Pray Until Something Happens", he said, and encouraged everyone to believe in prayer for God to do mighty things, not least in relation to my condition. Over those weeks, people sometimes asked, "What should we pray?" and I always said the same thing – "Please pray in faith for healing. Not for acceptance or resignation but for healing. Pray until something happens!"

We came home to celebrate Olivia's birthday, and she enjoyed opening her presents. Then we went down to Nicky's coffee place, Cafe Crème, in Newcastle town, which serves some of the best food and coffee we've ever had! We had a lovely time there, and as I watched her blowing out the seven candles on her cake, my mind drifted back to the night she was born in the Jubilee Maternity Hospital in Belfast, following that fast drive to get there in time. Having given birth to three boys, both of us had assumed that this would be the case again. I could still see clearly the look of joy on William's face as the midwife said "It's a girl – you have a little girl." "Did you say girl?" I said, "But I don't do girls!" Oh the joy that filled my heart!

The following morning William was dispatched to the nearest Mothercare store with orders to, "Go and buy everything in pink!" As I waited for him to come in I lay in my hospital bed looking across at my lovely little girl sleeping peacefully in the cot beside me, I was thinking about all the things we would do together as mum and daughter as she grew up. She was so beautiful, and bringing her home to Bangor in her Moses basket was one of the happiest days of my life.

We had originally thought only of boys' names, but one day having a coffee in Bangor's wonderful Café Brazilia, William said, "OK, I know we only ever seem to have boys especially right through my family, but if our baby turned out to be a girl, what would you name her?" Well, I hadn't thought about that, but when I did, I didn't hesitate at all. "Oh that's no problem," I had said, "I would name her Olivia!" The 'original' Olivia was one of my very best friends, now a Senior Nurse living in Colorado Springs. "Olivia Sharyn!" said William, and we had both laughed because we never really expected it to happen.

Of course, we love each of our boys, but Olivia was and still is a wonderful blessing to the whole family. Now I was facing the possibility of leaving her so young and it really hurt to the core of my being. "No way," I reminded myself, "by His stripes I am healed, I'm still claiming that verse every day."

The words, "Mummy, mummy, have some of my birthday cake!" brought me back from my memories and thoughts to the reality of the day, but I joined in determined not to take anything away from Olivia's special day.

It had taken a lot out of me both physically and emotionally, and I came home feeling quite exhausted. I glanced at our local newspaper the "Mourne Observer" and saw that there was a notice on the churches' page about the service of testimony that Steven had mentioned. However, William had a regular evening service and the boys were all going out so I didn't give it any further thought. Instead I decided to go to bed for a few hours while Olivia played with her new gifts, perhaps sleep would help to ease the heartache I was feeling as Monday's appointment drew nearer. As I got into bed I read through Psalm 91 again, and laid down to rest once more under the shadow of His wings.

When I was in bed Mr O'Brien telephoned to say that he was aware that I had been called for the appointment the next day and told William that the consultant we would be seeing was really good and would do the best that could be done for me, which was very re-assuring.

Later, William popped into the room just as I was waking up, and told me that Aidan had called. I said that was very kind of him as it was a Sunday afternoon, and that I had decided to go to the Elim service that evening. A quick phone call established that Donna could pick me up, and Olivia and I set off for Newcastle Elim, while William went to take the evening service in the Methodist Church at the other end of town.

I hadn't heard of Jean Neil before, and wasn't sure what to expect at the service, but I knew that the praise would be good and it was lovely just to be there with Olivia. There was another Abundant Life song written by Lara Martin that the worship group had learned, and they sang it especially for me that evening. Called "Divine Exchange", it captured what I was beginning to understand about God's healing power.

> "... He breaks the chains of sickness with authority,
> restoring what was broken.
> so it may fly again ...
> I live to worship you,
> I breathe to worship you,
> All of my days,
> Your face I will seek ..."

That was just what I needed to hear, I was feeling broken inside, and needed God to put me back together again, and I was still learning that seeking him each day in worship and His Word was part of that process. He is the one with all authority on heaven and on earth, and He could indeed restore what was broken.

Pastor Steven introduced Jean, who was from Rugby, in England. She said that she wanted to show a video before she shared her story. As it played on the screen, we could see it was a Reinhardt Bonnke conference which had been held in England a number of years before. Then we watched in amazement as we saw her get up out of her wheelchair and begin to walk, and then run across the platform. Olivia turned to me and said, "Look Mummy, Jesus healed that lady!" The video stopped rolling and the children left for their own meeting. As she began to speak I realised that she was not only going to share her experience, but would also be asking people to come for prayer at the end. I hesitated, as I hadn't expected that to happen. I just thought I would be listening to an encouraging story.

I waited for a while, and in response to an invitation from Jean, I found myself going forward for prayer. I felt such a strong compulsion to respond to what I had heard and knew that if I stayed in my seat and went home without prayer, then I would regret it.

Jean came and stood in front of me and asked why I had come forward. The tears ran down my cheeks as I told her that I would be going to an appointment the next day, when a doctor would tell me the results of my scans and whether I would live or die. Jean replied, "Sharyn, I believe that you coming here this evening is a Divine Appointment." Then she laid hands on me and particularly prayed against fear in my life. As she prayed, I felt the power of the Lord come over me in a way I never had before.

For the next half an hour or so God ministered to me in a very special way. Again the tears came, but this time they were in response to a great sense of peace flowing over and through me. I could hear the people praying around me but felt quite apart from them, I was so focused on the Lord. Then I began to hear Him speaking to me, for the first time in my life in this way. I know that I had experienced the Lord revealing things through reading His Word, perhaps seeing a verse that I may have read many times before suddenly coming alive when I needed it, but never like this. It was like a still small voice, not audible so that those around me could hear it, but forming thoughts in my mind that could be clearly understood. They are words I will never forget,

> *"You are not going to die, you are going to live. I am going to heal you and you will live to share this with many people. Do not look to man. I will supply all your needs."*

By then William had arrived and he came up to me at the top of the church. I shared with him what had happened in the service, and particularly what the Lord had said to me. Donna commented that unlike when I came in, I now had a smile on my face, a look of peace really, that matched how I was feeling inside.

We went away from there so strengthened and encouraged by those words, although not understanding the full significance of all of them at that time. The next day, however, was to be one of the hardest I would ever have to walk through, and one that would test my faith to the full.

16

THE LONGEST DAY

It used to be a day that had only one meaning on our family calendar – it was my father-in-law's birthday. We would laugh and say to him, "Trust you to get the most out of your birthday by having it on the longest day of the year", for that's how it's known in this part of the world.

But the 21st of June 2004 was to be my longest day for a totally different reason. It was to be the day when I would be told the results, of my latest scans. A day that would be a matter of life or death ...

We got up early that morning and spent sometime reading the Word together and chatting about all that had happened over the weekend, and the service that I had been to the night before.

Following lunch in Nicky's we drove to Musgrave Park Hospital, arriving at 1.25, in good time for the appointment. As we sat in the general waiting area we came to our scheduled time of 1.50 and still weren't called, I began to feel quite anxious and weak. "I don't think I can go through with this," I said, but we stayed there, and a nurse showed us into a room at 2.20, where we were to wait for the consultant to arrive.

To this day William can remember every detail of that room – even down to the blue carpet with a small speckled pattern on it!

I waited with William in the room when the consultant came in with a nurse, sat down, and placed a file on the small table in front of us, his head bowed almost apologetically. He began to speak very quietly, so quietly that we strained to hear exactly what he was saying, not wanting to miss any detail of his prognosis.

"I'm here to talk about the management of your tumours," he began. I wondered what he meant by 'management'. Surely there was to be some course of treatment, some type of operation, some hope medically for my condition?

Slowly he shook his head, and explained that the cancer was deemed to be inoperable, and my condition was terminal. Treatment was unlikely to work, but even if it did, it would only add a matter of weeks to my life.

I tried to take in what he was saying. "A couple of months?" I said, "A couple of months onto what? How much time do I have?"

"I'll tell you if you really want to know" he replied. I felt somehow suspended in time. Lots of thoughts flashed through my mind in an instant. I wondered if he was talking in terms of years. Would I have time to see the children growing up? Would William and I see our next wedding anniversary? His next words would determine all of that. Did I really want to know the answer to my own question?

"Yes," I blurted out, almost involuntarily. "Yes, I want to know – how long do I have?"

"A year at the most," he said. "I'm sorry." His words cut through me like a knife. I collapsed into William's arms – I knew the news might not be good, but I had no idea that it would be quite this bad.

The consultant left the room to go and get another file, when the nurse, who hadn't said anything up to that point, came over to us. She had been listening very carefully to what he had said, and as we made eye contact I could see that I hadn't misheard anything.

She asked me if there was anything that she could do. "Just hug me," I sobbed. She put her arms around me and just held me as I cried. After a few minutes I sat down in my seat again, and then she said the most amazing thing – "Sharyn, God is still in control." What did you say?" I asked. She repeated, "The consultant is going on the medical evidence in front of him, but God is still in control, you can change nothing – He can."

"But the Lord has told me I'm going to live," I said. "Then you must hold on to that," said June.

William says that as we began to share together my whole body posture changed, it was as if I had almost curled up into a ball, full of fear and despair. Now, as I spoke out words of faith, I straightened up, standing tall and firm on another verse we had read in Psalm 118,

> *"I shall not die, but live,*
> *and declare the works of the Lord."* (verse 17)

The consultant came back into the room, and very kindly waited while June continued to encourage me to hold on to my faith in the Lord. She had experienced a difficult time with illness in her own family a few years before, but had seen the Lord bring healing to that situation.

After a while the consultant said a few more things to me, about the possibility of arranging counselling to help me come to terms with what I had just been told, but there was no hope in what he was saying, only acceptance of the inevitable. I thanked him very much for his help and concern, but didn't need to hear any more, I just wanted to get out of the room and the hospital as soon as possible.

I wrote in my journal that evening that the Lord had sent June to me that day as if he had sent an angel into the room. I speak to June occasionally and she told me that she had been away on a course for some time, and was only back on that day covering for a nurse who was on holiday. That particular clinic only happened once a month, and it was another year before she worked on it again. There's no doubt in my mind that God had put her there that day to give me the encouragement I needed to go on even in the face of such traumatic news. I still thank God for her willingness to go the extra mile that day.

When we drove back to Newcastle, our first stop was at Steve and Donna's house. William had phoned ahead to tell them what had happened, and when Donna opened the door, she just held me and we cried together as we tried to understand the enormity of what had been said in that hospital room. I learned to be on the receiving end of the verse which tells us to "weep with those who weep".

I asked Steven, "Why didn't I hear that I was healed today?" He said, "Sharyn, this wasn't your day, but hold on to what God has said to you, and remember what the nurse said – God is in control." We spent some time in prayer, and then headed down the road to Newcastle.

Before we got home, we called to be with Malcolm and Liz. They were shocked and upset to hear the news, and tried to comfort me as best they could. Another lady from the congregation called shortly after we arrived and came in to see how I was. Mabel was very upset too, and very sad to hear the latest news. Just being there helped so much, and gave me some 'breathing space' before I had to face the family at home.

That was the most difficult part – how do you tell your family that you have less than a year to live? But tell them we must, and they said they would do their best to believe with me as I would cling to the promises of God and claim my life with all my heart.

We felt that we wanted to take a stand on the Word that I had been given, and so decided to tell anyone else who asked that we were believing the Lord for my complete healing. After all, either the Lord moved miraculously, or I would be dead within the year, as the doctors had said. William circulated an email, inviting much prayer ...

22 June 2004, 02.27am

Dear friends,

The specialist cancer consultant told us today that he would give Sharyn a year at the most to live, and that treatment is not a realistic option.
We believe that the Lord is on the throne, and that He can, and will, heal Sharyn, as her life is in His hands. Our God is the God of the impossible, and He alone can do it.
We would really value your ongoing prayers at this time, as nothing short of a miracle will make a difference in this situation,
– That's Plan 'A', friends
– There is no Plan 'B'...

As my longest day ever was drawing to a close, and my emotions were doing somersaults, I reached for my journal, and I wrote these words into it ...

"In His time I will know that I am all clear and healed. Until then, I will walk with the Lord, and rely on Him to hold me up – It's not an easy walk."

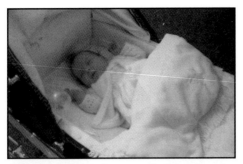

"Sheltered from the snow!" 1 March 1962

"Smiler Sharyn!" aged 1yr 9mths (1964)

Youth-camp '76 in Gurteen, aged 14

"Wedding Bells!" 16 May 1983

"Our Princess!" Olivia at 4 months, Oct '97

"All aboard for Ordination Day", Cork, June '99

"Heather's wedding" with Olivia, 19 June 2004

"Next stop Solihull" with Olivia, Evesham, 28 June 2004

"What would we do without Starbucks?!"
with Andy, Trafford Centre, August 2004

Baby William's first Christmas, 25 December 2004

Newcastle Methodist Church, Smiley Window with verse, "The Spirit also healeth our infirmities"

First media report – The Mourne Observer, 21 July 2004

With Mum, Dad, Rodney & Sylvia just before a speaking engagement in Dublin, February 2005

"Another day, another interview!" Media photo in Newcastle Manse, Easter 2005

One more that day by Bernie Brown, - Olivia with Topsy, Easter 2005

"Time moves on!" The family – Summer '99 and Christmas '04

17

DEATH IS NOT WELCOME HERE

William took some open-ended compassionate leave at that time, although he was still available for most of the regular Sunday Services and emergencies. My prognosis had given me less than a year to live, and the realistic view of most people was that it was only a matter of time, and we should have as much of that time as possible together as a family, nursing me whenever my condition deteriorated.

That option wasn't one that I was willing to consider. We wanted to use the time to get as close to the Lord as possible, to stand on the Word that I had been given, and to receive as much prayer as I could.

We had already made plans to go to stay with some friends in Cardiff on Thursday 24th June, returning on the following Tuesday, and I felt that we should go ahead with that plan. It would be good to get away for a while and spend some quality time together.

Early that week we were preparing to go when the phone rang. It turned out to be Inger Lannero, whom we had first met when she visited with the Alpha team in Portadown. We had been Alpha advisers for some time and were now members of the Northern Ireland Alpha Action Group, which was planning an Alpha Conference in Belfast the following June. I wanted to stay a part of the group, even though. medically speaking I shouldn't be still around when the planned conference was to happen.

After our last meeting at the Airport Conference Centre, when we shared my news with the group, Inger had led them in prayer for us before flying back to London, and had kept in touch regularly since. She worked with Alpha International, based in London at Holy Trinity Brompton and was the regional coordinator for all the Alpha advisers. The reason for her call was to find out our latest news.

When we told her, she said that she had recently had lunch with an Alpha adviser from Solihull. His name was Justin Marsh and he had told her some amazing stories of how God was working in miraculous ways in their church.

Inger said she felt it would be good if we could go there and gave us their website address so we could look at the details. We went into the study and found details of their regular Sunday services as well as the intriguingly titled "Ministry Of Power" weekly meeting, which was held on a Tuesday evening.

Our problem was that we were scheduled to fly home on the Tuesday afternoon and at this short notice it would cost a lot of money to change the flights, extend the car hire and book extra nights in the hotel. We wondered whether it would be worth it – after all, we had never heard of this place or these people before.

As we were discussing this, we heard a car pull up outside, and saw somebody walking past the study window. Then the doorbell rang. I recognised him as a retired man from our congregation. William invited him into the sitting room and he said that he had just called to see how I was doing as he had been away and hadn't heard the latest news.

We told him the prognosis and he didn't need to say anything; we could tell from his face that he knew how bad this was. I was feeling very upset and came up with some excuse to leave the room, and William stayed chatting with him for a while. After a short time he stood up to leave. He said that he was sorry that there was nothing he could do medically and then he slipped something into William's hand, saying, "Maybe you could take a holiday or something."

He wished us all the best and left. William looked down at his hand and was amazed to find a sum of money in English sterling notes which would be enough to cover changing our flight tickets, car hire, and hotel – all the additional expenses of staying for the Tuesday evening meeting in Solihull.

We thanked the Lord together, and took this as a clear indication that "The Ministry Of Power" was the place that God wanted us to be that night, so we made all the necessary amendments to the booking. Inger had suggested we call in advance, we phoned Pastor Justin but he was out of town. We left a message on his answering machine – trusting that he would get it in time.

The day before we left, we had arranged to go to see some folks that we had met briefly during our time in Cranagill. John and Doreen Greenaway are a wonderful couple who minister in healing from their base in the River of Life Fellowship just outside Portadown. They held a Wednesday evening meeting, and the speaker that evening was David Robinson who talked a lot about healing. I sat with my good friend Wendy Greenaway, whom I had known since we ministered in that area in our first church, and she had been a member of our ladies morning prayer group. It was a lovely time together, and both William and I received prayer that night.

We got home at 1am, and managed to grab a few hours sleep before getting up at 5.30 to drive to the airport for our flight to Liverpool. I felt that I was now very open to what the Lord wanted to do in my life. I knew it was going to be a special time, but I was still apprehensive about going. As I waited for the plane, I felt the Lord speaking to me, saying that I was about to get on an aeroplane, and entrust my life completely to that pilot, whom I didn't even know, to get me to my destination safely. How much more could I trust Him and put my life in His hands? Some verses then came to mind,

"Trust in the Lord with all your heart; and lean not on your own understanding. In all your ways acknowledge him, and he will direct your paths." (Proverbs 3:5-6)

We landed safely and smoothly, picked up the car and checked into the Trafford Centre Travel Inn where we were to stay for a couple of days before we went on to Cardiff. Early the following morning, William's mobile rang. It was Justin Marsh from Solihull.

He had been away at a conference and returned to find a message from us and an email from Inger, letting him know that we were hoping to come along to The Ministry of Power meeting that following Tuesday. He told us a little about Renewal Church, and then made arrangements to meet with us. We felt a lot happier now that we had some sort of contact with the place we had only seen on a website to date!

Thus far, we had seen the Lord's hand on our lives, as we acknowledged him, and we travelled down to Cardiff that Saturday to meet with our friends there. That evening they had arranged for another couple to come to dinner, and we settled Olivia down to sleep before having a lovely meal together.

Paul shared a little about the ministry of healing that he had been involved in, and as we finished the meal, he quoted a verse, the significance of which we had never really realised before. It was John 10:10,

"The thief comes only to steal, and to kill, and to destroy: I have come that they might have life, and that they might have it more abundantly."

It was like a revelation to me, despite the best efforts that were being made to steal, kill and destroy my life, Jesus was the only one who could offer real and abundant life.

Paul has a very wonderful ministry, and as he prayed with me, I knew that the Lord had moved in my life in a very personal and a very powerful way, and I experienced a great sense of freedom which has stayed with me ever since.

After a few more days we said our farewells and left Cardiff on Tuesday morning with an even greater sense of confidence and faith that I was being touched and set free by God's healing power, which continued to work in my life as I kept on claiming the promises in His Word.

At one stage we came off the motorway and stopped off at a small town called Evesham to have some lunch, and Olivia had some fun in the playground there. As she played we chatted about how good it was to know that Jesus still heals today. I was feeling quite nervous about going to a place I had never been before, to meet people I had never seen before. I'm sure that if William had suggested driving on back to Manchester avoiding Solihull, I probably would have agreed! On the other hand, we both knew that the Lord had provided the means for us to be there, rather than flying home that evening, so we put it out of our minds and carried on to where we had arranged to meet Pastor Justin, in the John Lewis department store!

We warmed to him right away as he came over with a big smile, enquiring if the journey had gone well and putting us at ease. He had made arrangements for us to go to the home of some church members for dinner, and we followed him to their house.

Steve and Karen welcomed us at the door and then she went on with the food preparations. As the children brought Olivia off to play, (and meet their hamsters!), Steve sat with us and shared his story.

After a while we realised why Justin had brought us to this particular home. A few years before Steve had been diagnosed with leukaemia, which was very aggressive indeed. Things were looking extremely bleak for him, but the folks at church were praying, and really believing for his healing. Lying in his hospital room, he was only allowed to nominate a couple of visitors to come and see him. He chose his wife Karen, and Pastor Dave Carr, Senior Minister of Renewal. Following regular prayer and laying on of hands, Steve astounded his doctors by totally recovering, and his healing remains firm to this very day.

As he shared about how he was restored to Karen and the children, the tears flowed down my cheeks, a regular occurrence in those days. I could feel faith rising up strong within me. Here was a person sitting in front of me who had cancer, and now they were well! It made such a difference to actually meet someone who had been through what I was going through, who had stared death in the face and seen it off through God's healing power. These days his son and some of the other young lads in Renewal have a Christian rock band with the great name "Death Is Not Welcome Here!" "Well," I thought, "if he can survive cancer through calling on the Name of Jesus, then I certainly can!"

We had some further fellowship over a beautiful meal, and then they offered to bring Olivia along to the meeting later, as Justin had arranged another meeting for us, half an hour before the main meeting was due to start. So it was that we arrived at Renewal Christian Centre and met up with Pastor Dave Carr for the first time.

18

AN ANGEL STOOD OVER ME

Although we had been a little apprehensive earlier in the day about coming to a strange place where we initially knew nobody, we knew that the Lord had provided the means, and our apprehension gave way to expectation, having heard what the Lord had done in Steve's life.

We followed Justin along Lode Lane and pulled into the large car park beside the Renewal building. He brought us up some stairs and we sat together on the comfortable leather seats in Pastor Dave's office. After a couple of minutes he came in and welcomed us. We had expected to have a very brief word with him, but he didn't seem in any hurry, and began to share with us all that God had been doing in his life and in the life of the Church up to this point, especially through the Tuesday evening meetings. As he was speaking, we both had an overwhelming sense that there was a lot more to this encounter than we would realise that evening.

At one point I wondered if Justin had actually told him what had been wrong with me at all, as I noticed that the time was getting closer and closer to the start time of 7.30. Suddenly, he asked me the strangest question that I certainly wasn't expecting. "Well, Sharyn," he said, "has God told you that you're going to die?" "Certainly not," I said, thinking about the word I had been given at the Elim service. "He has told me that I'm going to LIVE!" "Well, in that case we're going to pray for life," he said, "God is always faithful to His Word, you can be sure of that."

With that he glanced at his watch and said, "Time to go folks," and we headed down the stairs and into the main church. As we came in I noticed that there were lots of different flags hanging in the foyer. I found out later that each time a new nationality showed up at this multi-cultural church, they would put up the flag of their country. I had immediately noticed a Manx flag, which you don't see that often, and as my mum is from the Isle of Man there was a lovely familiarity about it. The second thing we noticed was the number of people, about seven or eight hundred, there for what had begun a few years before as a regular Tuesday evening prayer meeting. They were praising and worshipping the Lord, lifting up the name of Jesus in a mighty way.

The main thing that hit both of us was how the presence and power of God was so real in that place. We felt that we could literally reach out and touch it. In the days when William was a travel agent, we had visited some very hot countries, and the feeling as we walked into that atmosphere reminded us of the feeling we would get when the door opens on an air-conditioned 747, and the heat would almost take your breath away. It wasn't a physical heat, the temperature of the room was very comfortable – it was a powerful sense of the Lord's presence and glory as He was enthroned on the praises of His people.

Following a wonderful time of worship, Pastor Dave stood up to speak, and in a very simple and straightforward way shared about the power of Jesus to save and to heal, quoting from many of the verses that we had been reading over the previous few weeks. We took note of them,

Luke 4:40
"When the sun was setting, the people brought to Jesus all who had various kinds of sickness, and laying his hands on each one, he healed them."

Luke 5:15
"... the news about him spread all the more, so that crowds of people came to hear him and to be healed of their sicknesses."

Matthew 9:35
"Jesus went through all the towns and villages, teaching in their synagogues, preaching the good news of the kingdom and healing every disease and sickness."

As soon as he had finished reading these, he said, "Everywhere that Jesus set his foot, people were healed – You can be sure of this - when Jesus turns up in this place tonight, people WILL be healed."

Olivia had joined us when we arrived and she turned to me and said, "Did you hear that mummy, if Jesus comes here tonight – people will be healed!" As she had only just turned seven years old, although she knew I wasn't well, we had never told her just how bad her mummy's condition was. Now she had listened carefully, and with her simple child-like faith, she knew that if what Pastor Dave had said was true for all those people in the Bible, then it was true for her mummy too.

As the band began to lead worship again, he invited the people there to come to the front for healing, with any who were terminally ill to come forward first. It actually took me quite a few moments to realise that included ME! William came and stood alongside me as I went forward for prayer. Pastor Dave moved along the line of people, starting at the opposite end to where I was, anointing them with oil, and speaking words of healing into their lives.

There wasn't any shouting and yelling, just a deep sense of compassion for those who had gathered to put themselves under the mercy and grace of Jesus' healing power. When he got to where I was he didn't actually touch me at all, but simply rebuked the cancer in the name of Jesus. I certainly experienced an awesome sense of the power of God surging through me in an amazing way. I've heard Pastor Dave describe it since saying "Sometimes it's as if God showers you with His Spirit, other times it's more like taking a bath!"

The atmosphere of worship was beautiful and uplifting during this time and the simple words of one particular song seemed to capture the moment for me,

You deserve the glory,
and the honour;
Lord, we lift our hands
in worship,
as we lift your holy name.
You deserve the glory,
and the honour.
Lord, we lift our hands
In worship,
as we lift your holy name.

For you are great,
you do miracles so great

There is no one else like you,
there is no one else like you.
You are great,
you do miracles so great.
There is no one else like you,
there is no one else like you.

There were various other members of the healing ministry team who continued to pray and share with me, and as one lady laid hands on me and anointed me with oil I felt a tremendous heat flow through my head and into my body. I later found out that she was Molly Carr, Pastor Dave's lovely wife, who also has a wonderful ministry in this area. Kevin shared with me how his 12-year-old daughter had been healed of cancer, and had her planned operation cancelled when she proved to be clear after prayer.

William wasn't ignored either, as a man named Bob came alongside him, saying that he knew what it felt like to be a husband watching his loved one going through the experience of life–threatening cancer. His wife Wendy had also been healed, one of the first at this meeting a number of years before.

Justin continued to pray for me too, and I just found myself repeating the simple words over and over, "Lord, thank you for healing me, thank you for healing me."

After quite a while I returned to my seat and continued to thank and worship the Lord as many other people were receiving prayer. Then Olivia leaned over and said, 'Mummy, as you were at the front being prayed for I saw something up there." "What did you see love?" I said. She hesitated, and then came out with it, "Well, mummy, I saw an angel standing over you!" Olivia isn't given to making things up, and as she described what she saw, we realised that in a very special way through the eyes of a child, she had seen something in the spiritual realm to which we as adults are often blind. We have asked her since then, "Who told you it was an angel?" "Nobody told me," she said, "I just knew!" We continued to thank the Lord for His presence and power and were probably the last people to leave the building that night.

The memory of that Tuesday evening will continue to be very special to all of us in different ways, and we could see now why He had provided the means to go there in such an amazing way.

We thought about how all the teaching we had heard in the earlier part of the meeting had been based solidly on the Word of God, that Word which had now taken root within me and was going to bear fruit. We also thought of how Bob had come to pray with William, and how important it is to see how ministry is needed, not only to the one who has an illness but their surrounding family also, as they go through the trauma and pain with a loved one.

For my part, I know now in my heart that it was the time when God not only confirmed my healing, but also anointed me to pray for the sick. That would be for the future, but for now as we said goodbye to the folks at Renewal, and headed back up the M6 to Manchester, we knew we still had another road to travel, and it would not be an easy one.

19

MY FAITH JACKET!

We had another day before we travelled home, and we went to Starbucks in the Trafford Centre for a long chat about the events of the previous few days. I took out my journal and began to write down how I was feeling. I had a sense of peace that God had done His work in me – that the cancer had left my body. I know now that it was what is referred to in scripture as the "peace that passes understanding".

Medically, it made no sense – the words that had been spoken by my consultants hadn't changed at all, but I was standing in faith on the promises of His Word, and whenever I got home, I was determined to continue telling anyone who asked that I was believing for my total healing.

After coffee, I went for a walk around the centre, and William went to check for any emails that may have come in when we were away. I was standing looking at a couple of jackets when he walked into the shop. I turned to him and said, "This is crazy - why am I thinking about buying clothes? According to the doctors I won't be needing them – I should be giving away what I have got to a charity shop!" William laughed, "Hey, remember what we said about having a thanksgiving service whenever your healing is confirmed? Well, you'll need something to wear, won't you?" "Sure," I said, "I can't go turning up in any old thing!" "We'll call it your 'faith jacket'!" said William.

And so it was that I bought two jackets – my 'faith jackets' – to wear at some time, yet unspecified, to testify of my healing! It may seem like a trivial thing – but that's how convinced I was of God's healing power at work in my life. The jackets were like an outward physical representation of an inner sense that I was believing, really believing what I had confessed with my mouth and in my heart. When I got home, I hung the jackets in my wardrobe, wondering when I would have the opportunity to wear them - the next few days would reveal all.

We had previously received a letter from Mr O'Brien, which set out before us the next collection of appointments and scans which seemed to dominate our diaries and our lives. The letter informed me that I would be attending the Department of Radiology in Craigavon Area Hospital for further CT scanning of my chest, abdomen, and pelvis. They would also send me another appointment for a complete bone scan. I would be attending a Consultant Radiologist in Belvoir Park Hospital for MRI scanning of my chest and abdomen, and I would be seeing a Clinical Oncology Consultant there also.

Finally, at the end of all this, I would be meeting with Aidan himself on the 9th of July to review results of all the scans and consultations. The correspondence closed with the words, "I look forward to meeting with you once again." That's nice, I had thought, as I put the letter down, but I wondered what that meeting would hold in store for me.

When I had read that letter I knew that every scan, every appointment I had attended so far, had brought news which had continued to go from bad to worse, but I had grown in my faith and was now putting my ultimate trust for my well-being in the Lord. As the next set of appointments that had been scheduled would come along one by one, I was determined to hold on to that sense of peace that I had experienced in those special times of encounter with Him.

I was also beginning to understand that being open to hearing His Word was less dependent on being in a particular place and more on being aware and open to Him at any time and in any place.

Although Psalm 91 was my greatest source at that time, other Psalms also spoke to me, and one of these was Psalm 40. David seemed to capture where I had been for some time, in a pit crying out to God, but recognising that his deliverance from it was not just an action which would save him, but would help others to see God's power and put their trust in Him also.

> *"I waited patiently for the Lord;*
> *he turned to me and heard my cry.*
> *He lifted me out of the slimy pit,*
> *out of the mud and mire;*
> *he set my feet on a rock*
> *and gave me a firm place to stand.*
> *He put a new song in my mouth,*
> *a hymn of praise to our God.*
> *Many will see and fear,*
> *and put their trust in the Lord."* (verses 1-3)

I received a letter quite recently questioning why, when I had been given the bad news, I hadn't simply acknowledged the fact that as a Christian I was going to heaven. If I was going to die, I should settle for that and be glad of it, or I should have been patient, sat back, and accepted whatever came my way.

We could see that despite David's many shortcomings, the Lord responded to his cries for help, because he was a man after God's own heart. Somehow David had to find a balance between "waiting patiently", and realising that his life-threatening situation called for immediate action, so he threw himself on God's mercy knowing that He alone could deliver him. A few verses later he wrote,

> *"Be pleased, O Lord to save me,*
> *O Lord, come quickly to help me"* (verse 13)
> *"... You are my help and my deliverer;*
> *O my God, do not delay."* (verse 17b)

It seemed to us that there was plenty of evidence in Scripture that God wanted us to take a firm hold of all His promises, and believe the truth of them. That's why He gave them to us in the first place. Nevertheless, I'm only human, I still had to battle with my fears and emotions through those days, and I certainly didn't look forward with any degree of relish to the scans that stretched before me.

It was Friday 2nd July and I was sitting in the hospital canteen drinking the fluid that has to be absorbed before a full MRI scan is done. The orange flavour didn't really disguise the awful taste at all, but I knew that I needed to go through these scans for a purpose. I could feel the Lord's presence, assuring me of His love, protection and deliverance because I had called upon His name.

Over the weekend, I tried to relax and stay focused on the Lord, reading my healing verses, and also getting on with doing some normal things around the house. I knew that Monday would be a long day with the bone scan scheduled, so I watched some faith-building programmes and went to bed quite early on Sunday evening.

As we drove over to the hospital, I was feeling quite drained emotionally that day, and found it hard to lift myself up with the prospect of going through it all again. When I arrived, I had to wait for a while and then I was given an injection in preparation for the scan. Usually we would have gone to the hospital canteen but on this day the prospect of sitting around for all that time wasn't very appealing. I had an idea and rang my friend Wendy who didn't live too far from the hospital. She had said that anytime I wanted to call, she would love to see me.

It was a really nice time of fellowship with one of the few people that had really stood with me in believing for my healing from the very first day of my prognosis. Wendy and my other close friend Christine had sent me texts with encouraging verses every day, which meant so much to me.

Wendy seemed to be able to understand the mixed emotions that I was feeling. I was absolutely believing God for my healing, and yet at times tears just seemed to come from nowhere. She encouraged me as we sat and shared together the healing scriptures that I had been reading, and recounted to her what had happened to me over the previous few days.

As the time came to head back to the hospital, she hugged me close and whispered words of encouragement to me, saying that she would continue to pray, and expect good news soon!

20

ONLY BELIEVE

When we got back to the Radiology Department there was some sort of problem, and they weren't ready to take me at the appointed time. I squeezed William's hand tightly as we waited, feeling quite upset at the delay, even though I had been around hospitals long enough to know that these things can't be helped. When the time came to be called, William assured me that he would be sitting right outside the door.

As I went in, the nurse helpfully began to give directions as to what to do, but I was by now all too familiar with scanning rooms and their procedures. This scan was going to take some time and she told me that I should keep my eyes closed for the duration. I lay down and waited for it to begin, vaguely aware of some soft music playing in the background.

After a while I became aware of a deep sense of the Lord speaking words of life to me in the stillness:

"I love you, I know what you have been through. I have seen your tears and your heartache. Do not fear, my arms are around you, it is over. This is just a piece of machinery to prove your healing to others, and I will use you to help other people that are hurting."

I didn't want that scan to end! It was such a precious time, as if I was literally bathing in the Lord's presence. I came out of the scanning room to find William waiting for me and I couldn't wait to tell him what had happened. When I had finished I said to him, "But how can I be sure that was the Lord speaking to me, how do I know they weren't just my thoughts?"

William replied, "Look, you've had a really difficult day emotionally. If anything, you went in there feeling quite down and drained, even a bit negative – they were not the sort of thoughts you would have been thinking." On the way home in the car he added to that, "There's one sure way to know if it was the Lord's voice you heard – if it was, and I believe it was – it will happen just as he said!"

Those words had come so clearly to me that although I wrote them into my journal when I got home, I don't really need to look them up, I will never forget them. I added some words of my own "Thank you, Lord, for that still small voice of encouragement, just when I needed it."

I was taking steps of faith, and praying prayers of faith, as it says in James 5:15,

> *"The prayer of faith shall save the sick,*
> *and the Lord shall raise him up."*

I had known little or nothing about what verses like that meant in Scripture but now I was grasping onto them with both hands, and taking them at face value.

William would often quote how the author Mark Twain reacted when he was asked whether it worried him that there were parts of the Bible he couldn't understand. He gave a great reply,

"It ain't those parts of the Bible that I can't understand that bother me, it's the parts that I DO understand!"

My understanding was that the more I looked at Scripture the more it seemed to say in a very simple way – Jesus heals, and that fact hasn't changed today.

Over the next few days I felt very strongly that I should tell people that I had been healed, not that I wanted to be, or hoped to be, but that I actually was healed, and that the Lord had set me free from cancer. It wasn't that I went looking for folks to tell, but when I did meet folks, or receive a telephone call, that was what I did and the response I got was very varied indeed.

Those close friends and family who had been believing and standing with us for my healing accepted what I said without hesitation, but for many I knew by their response, whether it was a slightly stammered reply of "Oh yes?", or a silence at the other end of the telephone, that they simply believed that I was in denial.

I'm not going to criticise anybody for having that reaction to me. At the end of the day, I probably would have thought that myself not too many months before. I have always said that the hardest ones to say it to were our children. Somewhere in the back of my mind were the questions, "What if I've got it wrong? What if it doesn't work out?" I could feel an enormous sense of responsibility for the effect that it would have on their faith in the future should I say one thing, and another should happen. However, I knew what I had to do, I had to be faithful to God as

He had been faithful to me, I had to rebuke those thoughts in the name of Jesus, and put my whole trust in Him.

I'm happy to say that I WAS in denial alright, but not in the way a lot of people were thinking. I never denied that, medically speaking, my situation was terminal and without hope. I never denied that the medical prognosis was anything but correct – there were too many hospitals, scans, radiographers and consultants involved to even think of doing that. If any medical treatment had been offered to me, I would not have denied them the opportunity to carry it out – of course, that option was never there.

However, I denied that I had to give in to the cancer that was trying to take my life, and I denied that the promises of healing in God's Word were anything less than true. Paul wrote to Timothy about a type of denial – he said the days were coming when people would be,

> *"holding to a form of godliness, but denying its power"* (2 Timothy 3:5)

I didn't want to be one of those people that denied God's power, and when I read again the words of John 10:10

> *"The thief comes only to steal, kill and destroy, but I have come that you might have life, and have it abundantly."*

I denied that anyone but God was in total control of my situation and He had told me that I was going to live!

The important thing for me to do at that time was see what Jesus himself did, even in the most difficult of circumstances, when Jairus brought news of his dying daughter to Him. His power was sufficient to meet even that need,

" ... But Jesus hearing it, answered him, Fear not, only believe, and she shall be made whole." (Luke 8:50)

If there was one thing I knew, it was that I needed His power in my life, I needed to rebuke the fear that would come upon me, and I needed to believe by faith that He would fulfil the promises of His Word in my life, and I would be made whole.

So that was the way I chose to live my live, absolutely trusting that Jesus was just as capable of doing in these days what he had always done. Any morning during this time when I woke up and just didn't feel like getting out of bed, William would say to me, "Don't give Satan another day – this is the day that the Lord has made!" I would get up, get washed and dressed, and claim life, in the face of death.

One day, William's mum and dad had come up from Dublin on the bus to spend the day with us and give me some encouragement. As they were about to leave, she put something in my hand. "I got this especially for you," she said, "to hang on the kitchen window." When I looked down I saw that it was a beautiful piece of round stained glass with the words "Faith Can Work Miracles" on it. Whenever I looked out the window, I could see these words in front of me, and they were so encouraging. In fact, it still hangs on my kitchen window today.

It had been a long week, and on Thursday afternoon, the day before I was due to get my latest series of results, I wrote this prayer in my journal,

"Thank you, Jesus, that you have healed and delivered me. I claim this today, I know that I will get clear results tomorrow. Thank you for doing this for me and my family. I want to witness to many people this wonderful thing that you have done which the doctors said was not possible. All things are possible, only believe - Lord, I believe." - 8th July 2004, 4.15pm.

21

NOT THAT I KNOW OF

The next morning we took the long drive over to Craigavon Area Hospital, playing some worship CDs in the car, and I thanked the Lord for my healing all the way there. We pulled into the car park with a few minutes to spare, and sat for a while, reflecting on all the things that had happened since that first call to the doctor-on-call back in April 2003.

I had learned so much from the Word about God's healing power that I just hadn't known, or understood before, but most of all I now knew deep down in my heart that He really loved me and that He KNEW me, as an individual, not just as a name or a number. As long as I can remember, my favourite Bible verses had always been the words of Jesus in Matthew chapter 6. As I waited to go in to the hospital, I realised that they had taken on a whole new significance for me during this time, and especially as I had read it the night before.

"Therefore I tell you, do not worry about your life, what you will eat or drink; or about your body, what you will wear. Is not life more important than food, and the body more important than clothes? Look at the birds of the air; they do not sow or reap or store away in barns, and yet your heavenly Father feeds them. Are you not much more valuable than they? Who of you by worrying can add a single hour to his life?... seek first his kingdom and his righteousness, and all these things will be given to you as well. Therefore do not worry about tomorrow, for tomorrow will worry about itself." (25-27; 33-34)

Now tomorrow had come, and I was facing it in faith, albeit a little nervously! We made a last call to some friends who prayed with us before we went in to the hospital.

The purpose for this appointment had been to review all the latest scans, and check the progression of the tumours. We assumed that from the medical standpoint that information would make it possible to have a clearer indication as to how long I had left to live – perhaps even less than the year that had been stated, depending on how aggressive it was.

The ever-polite Monica directed us to a seat near to Mr O'Brien's room. I suppose we were only sitting there for five or ten minutes, but it seemed like an age.

Suddenly he came around the corner with a big smile on his face, and directed us towards the door of his office. As we stood up, I thought to myself, "What's he smiling for? He hasn't smiled around me for months!" As we walked into the office he turned to me and said, "Sharyn, I feel that you are going to leave this hospital a happier girl than you came in today!"

We could see that he was about to start going through my very large medical file so I said, "Am I going to die?" "No!" he said, with an even broader smile, "not that I know of anyway!"

William and I hugged each other with relief. Inside I just kept saying, "Thank you, Lord, I'm going to live" but I also knew there would be plenty of time to celebrate later; now we turned to examine the file, we wanted to know what had happened.

We sat there as Aidan explained how three world authorities in Glasgow, London, and Harvard had examined the tumour and had confirmed that the cancer cells which were examined were indeed a rare form of Spindle Cell Sarcoma, usually found in the bones.

He went on to say that all the scans had been collated and examined the previous day, and the radiographer was quite taken aback by what he saw, or rather by what he didn't see! Three other radiographers had been called in to examine them, and then they went back over the previous scans also.

They could clearly see the progression of the lesions and tumours that had taken place, first on my kidney and then on my lungs. But on the latest set of scans that had just been taken, they had stopped. In fact the lung, kidney and bone scans now showed no trace of the cancer at all, I was completely clear!

Because he had been so honest with us when it came to the bad news, we knew that we could trust him impeccably when he gave us this good news. Aidan was almost as pleased as we were, and as we shook hands with him, we thanked him warmly for all his wonderful attention since Easter 2003.

We talked for another while and then we left the hospital with such joy for we knew that God had been faithful to His Word!

We had lots of phone calls to make, to family and friends. I rang Donna and William rang Steven at the same time, and my brother Rodney was so happy for me. William got through to Pastor Dave, who was shouting down the phone with delight, and then prayed with us, that God would use this wonderful news to His glory. Some of the calls were really funny, such as the friend I rang and shouted down the phone, "It's Sharyn - I'm healed, I'm healed." "You're what?" she said, "could you run that by me again?" "Oh, that's just great," I said, "you kept telling me to believe for my healing, and now you're in total shock that it's happened!" Of course, we rejoiced together and have laughed about that call many times since!

I rang Andy and said, "It's happened, I have my miracle!" Both he and Kelvin were delighted, and I was so glad that I had taken that step of telling them when the Lord had told me to.

We went out for lunch to Alexanders of Markethill, one of our favourite places, a few miles from the hospital. We were feeling so grateful to the Lord, and I'm sure the staff wondered why we never stopped smiling the whole time that we were there!

After lunch we drove back to Newcastle and called into Malcolm and Liz. They were so happy and relieved and held me tightly, but for a very different reason than the time we had arrived there with our bad news.

When I had been ill, I had said to William one day, "Whenever I get news of my healing, there's something that I want to do. It's just a silly thing I know, but I want to walk on the beach in the rain!"

We went down to the beach, but it wasn't raining. As we were walking along, I decided to try and contact Justyn again. He was away on a two-week camp in England, and it had been difficult to get in touch with him, but as we walked on the beach I managed to get through on the mobile.

I told him what had happened, and in typical teenage fashion, he just kept saying, "Wow, this is SO cool!" We were really pleased that at least for the second week of his camp, he wouldn't have the thought of his mum's serious illness to cope with.

When I had finished on the phone, we walked along Newcastle beach, admiring the beauty of God's creation - the sand, the sky, the mountains, and the sea. We could see our church on the Central Promenade clearly, and thought of a song that we had been using regularly at the 8.30 services.

> *Shout to the Lord all the earth*
> *let us sing,*
> *Power and majesty, praise*
> *to the King.*
> *Mountains bow down and*
> *the seas will roar,*
> *at the sound of Your name.*
>
> *I sing for joy at the work of Your hands.*
> *Forever I'll love you,*
> *forever I'll stand.*
> *Nothing compares to the promise I have in You.*

© Darlene Zschech / Hillsongs

As we walked, I had a sense of the power of the Lord, and the faithfulness of His promises. As if to complete the picture, it began to rain! As the beach cleared with other people heading for cover, we simply looked up, let the water run down our faces, and rejoiced together in what God had done in my life.

22

IT'S ONLY A NAME!

I woke up on Saturday and lay in bed for a few minutes thinking about all the things that had happened over the previous weeks and months. It was difficult enough to take in.

It was a brand new day, and in many ways a brand new life. I thanked the Lord again and again for the news that I had received, and thought about the different people that the Lord had used to minister to me. In some cases it was prayer ministry, with others it was simply an email, a card, a text message or a brief word of encouragement over the telephone.

The rain had stopped and we went for another walk along the beach that day. We talked about how it felt to see the fulfillment of the Lord's Word in my life, and reflected on how the healing verses had worked in me.

As Proverbs 4:20-24 said, I had listened to His words, and kept them in my heart … and they were, quite literally, to me life and health –

22 *"For they are life to those who find them
And health to all their body."*

Alongside reading my healing verses, and spending a lot of time in worship and prayer, I had also gone for prayer ministry when the opportunity arose. One of the things that concerned me at the time was whether asking for prayer more than once was perhaps displaying a lack of faith – surely I should ask once and leave it at that. The Psalmist came to mind again, there seemed to be no hesitation there in returning to the Lord regularly seeking answers to prayer, and then Jesus himself told a parable about persisting in prayer.

I recalled the day, just after my bad prognosis, when my own GP, Dr John Kyle, who is a lovely Christian man, came to visit me at home.

Things were looking very bleak at the time and I was very upset as we discussed what the medical outlook might be. Even so, I said that I believed that God was going to heal me.

As he was about to leave, he noticed a wall hanging which we had put there only a few weeks before. It said, 'Life is fragile, handle with prayer.' He pointed to it and said, 'Well, the first part of that is so true, and the second part is what we all need to do.'

He was so pleased whenever the news of my healing came through, and I'm thankful to him for his care for me and all the family.

Around that time, a few weeks before my healing was confirmed, William was having a meeting with Steven and some other ministers at Nicky's coffee shop – where else?! They had both arrived a little early, and he mentioned this concern about regular prayer to Steven. He said, "Actually, I felt that I should share this word with you today – Namaan. Go and have a look at what happened to Namaan when you get home." He didn't answer William's question, the Word would do that.

It was a story that we vaguely remembered from our Sunday School days, certainly William had never used it as a sermon topic, but we found it in 2 Kings 5, and as we read afresh what had happened, we could feel the Lord speaking to us through the pages.

When Namaan went to the prophet Elisha with his leprosy looking for healing, he was told to go and dip in the Jordan seven times. Reluctant at first, he argued that if he was going to dip in any river, it would be in his homeland of Syria, apparently the rivers were cleaner there! The point was made to him that if he had been asked to do some amazing feat to receive his healing, he would have done it without hesitation. Then he was challenged to do this very simple thing, and when he finally gave in to the Lord's word for him, the result was that he was totally healed, the leprosy left his body, and his skin was like that of a young boy.

The healing didn't happen on the first, third, or fifth time that he dipped in the Jordan, only on the seventh. This record of what happened all those years ago isn't a formula for healing, nor is seven just a lucky number, nor does everyone who has a swim in the Jordan get healed. It's a story about obedience. Healing came to Namaan when he showed that he was willing to be obedient to whatever God's prophet told him to do. As God provided the opportunity to receive, he had taken it up, just as I had done over the previous weeks when I sought healing prayer.

In those days the word "leprosy" was enough to strike terror into the hearts of those who heard it. It was a word without hope, a disease without cure. It was a word much like the word "cancer" is today. Thankfully, due to the advances in medical science, leprosy is under control, and some wonderful research is being carried out in the fight against cancer in these days.

There are many kinds of treatment available, and we thank God for it, and for the many doctors, nurses and consultants who administer it. Ultimately, I believe that all healing comes from the Lord, whatever way it comes.

However, in my case there was no treatment, there was no operation, there was no hope given to me. I was facing a situation where all the money in the world couldn't have made any difference to the news that I had been given.

As we read together about the many times that Jesus healed people, we began to realise that there is a marked differerence in the way the people reacted to Him then, and now. It seemed that it was generally accepted that Jesus could heal and deliver people all around him as he carried out His earthly ministry; for example, in Matthew chapter 8,

> *"When evening came, many who were possessed were brought to him, and he drove out the spirits with a word and healed all who were sick. This was to fulfil what was spoken through the prophet Isaiah:*
> *"He took up our infirmities*
> *and carried our diseases."* (verses 16-17)

The religious leaders of the day didn't seem to have a problem with the fact that He could do all of this. Their problem was that He dared to say He could forgive sins, and that meant He was the Son of God.

When I was ill, I could see a complete reversal of this in these days. Many people seemed to have no problem at all with the idea that Jesus can and does forgive sins, but the idea that He might still be in the ministry of healing and delivering people today seemed to pose a great problem for them.

I took these words at face value and applied them to my life,

> *"Jesus Christ the same yesterday, and today, and forever."* (Hebrews 13:8)

Jesus hadn't and wouldn't change. If He could do all of those things then, then surely He could do all of those things now. I couldn't see a line drawn anywhere that said He stopped, quite the opposite. He called His disciples together and told them,

> *"Truly, I say to you, He who believes in me, the works that I do shall he do also; and greater works than these shall he do; because I go unto my Father."* (John 14:12)

It seemed to us that Jesus had expected His work on this earth to go on, even after He had ascended to His Father – that's why the Holy Spirit came, as promised by Him.

During my illness, there was a particularly special word which the Lord gave to me, and which I want to pass on to you, the reader of this book. Paul wrote to the Phillipians,

> *"Therefore God exalted Him to the highest place, and gave Him the name that is above every name, that at the name of Jesus every knee should bow, in heaven, and on earth, and under the earth; and every tongue confess that Jesus Christ is Lord, to the glory of God the Father."* (2:9-11)

Because of what Jesus did, God raised Him and gave to Him the Name that is above every other name. As I was claiming my healing by faith in God's Word, it came to me - "Jesus is the name above all names. Cancer is only a name, and Jesus' name is above cancer."

I don't share this with you lightly – I know what cancer can do to a body – what it was doing to my body. But it was a truth that changed my life. It gave me a real understanding of what

Jesus had achieved for me on the cross, taking both my sin *and* my sickness.

Coming up off the beach we went for coffee and met some folks there who asked how I was doing. I suppose that was when I first realised how words are so inadequate to express the amazing thing that God had done in my life. I also realised that even with my scan results there would be some who would be pleased that I was well but sceptical as to the reasons why.

Joanna from the Elim church worked there and just smiled across the counter as she handed us our coffee. She had no such doubts at all. "Didn't we know the Lord could do it?!", she said.

Yes, indeed we did!

We went home that day and read Psalm 20 together, words that we had proven to be true in my own life, and they can be just as true for yours,

> 4 *May he give you the desire of your heart*
> *and make all your plans succeed.*
> 5 *We will shout for joy when you are victorious*
> *and will lift up our banners in the name of our*
> *God.*
> *May the LORD grant all your requests.*
> 6 *Now I know that the LORD saves his anointed;*
> *he answers him from his holy heaven*
> *with the saving power of his right hand.*
> 7 *Some trust in chariots and some in horses,*
> *but we trust in the name of the LORD our God ...*

23

RELEASED FROM CAPTIVITY

The following Sunday morning 11th July, William was conducting the service, and oh!, what a different atmosphere was there that day. He invited me to get up and share what had happened to me and how prayer had been answered. I suppose that I had better explain here that I wasn't a speaker at all at that time. As a Methodist minister's wife I would do an appropriate devotion at the beginning of the monthly ladies meeting, which involved a short reading and a prayer, but that was it! On occasion William might ask me to do a prayer or a reading somewhere, and I would only agree if he convinced me that he had absolutely no one else to ask!

As Alpha Advisers, we would run conferences, courses and training seminars, but I was very much the administrator, keeping everything running smoothly, yes – but behind the scenes, apart from making announcements to make sure everyone knew what they were doing. William was the one up front, doing the speaking, leading the worship, and I was quite happy to keep it that way.

We worked as a team, and still do, but God was beginning to do something in me that I never would have expected. There was no way out on that Sunday morning! If I was sitting there, it didn't make any sense for him to tell my story, I just had to get up and do it. The good thing was, of course, that these were our church family, the folks who had been around during the time all this had been happening, so apart from some summer visitors I knew that I would know most of the people there, and that made it a little bit easier.

We began by singing,

"To God be the glory,
Great things he has done..."

I don't think I had ever heard it sung with more conviction and joy than that morning. I stood up after a while and shared very briefly what had happened to me, and I don't think there was a dry eye in the house when I had finished. Suddenly, one man began to clap, and the rest of the congregation joined him in spontaneous applause. It was their way of showing their joy and saying "thank you" to God for what He had done in my life. William later announced that if it was possible, we were hoping to plan a service of thanksgiving at the 8.30 on the next available Sunday evening. All would be welcome to come, and we hoped that we might have a few friends along who had prayed for Sharyn also.

The following Tuesday afternoon Pastor Justin called from Renewal. He asked me if I could do a live-link telephone interview that evening with the Ministry of Power service in Solihull. I agreed and at about 8pm the phone rang.

I tried not to think about the fact that as I was sitting with William in my living room being interviewed by Justin and

Pastor Dave Carr, there were about 800 people listening over the sound system at the other end! It was the first time I had shared my story in any real detail, but it just seemed to flow out of me.

I could visualise myself there only a few weeks before, and when I put the phone down, I said to William, "Well, I just hope and pray that I helped even one person who felt how I was feeling when I was there that day." We prayed together that this would be the case.

The next day we had an email from Justin, telling us that, following the interview, a number of people had given their lives to the Lord and many received prayer for healing from cancer and many other forms of sickness. It had been my first experience of speaking to a large gathering, although it didn't feel that way over the telephone. But, even more significantly, those people coming to Christ were the first fruit of a new ministry to which God was calling me, but it would be a little while before I began to realise this myself.

Now that I had been given the good news that all was well medically, we felt that we wanted to spend a few days 'away from it all'. On the Wednesday morning we booked into a nice hotel in Avoca, County Wicklow. It was somewhere that I often visited and is a small village best known as the location where the BBC television programme Ballykissangel was filmed. For us, it was simply a quiet place where we could spend some quality time together, relaxing, praying, and seeking the Lord for what He would have us do next. It was a lovely few days as we started to try to come to terms with all that we had been through, and the fact that now we did have a future together, thanks to the Lord's healing power. We remembered some verses from Jeremiah 29:11,

"For I know the plans I have for you," declares the LORD,

plans to prosper you and not to harm you,
plans to give hope and a future.
Then you call upon me, and come and pray to me,
and I will listen to you.
You will seek me and find me
 when you seek me with all your heart
"I will be found by you", declares the Lord,
"and will release you from your captivity."

Even though these words were written thousands of years ago about God's relationship with His people in exile, they had come alive for us in 2004. My mind went back to Lara's Martin's song, Divine Exchange, which I had first heard the night before the 21st of June,

"... He breaks the chains of sickness with authority,
restoring what was broken,
so it may fly again."

Oh, how grateful I was to the Lord for His healing and restoring power in my life, and now we wanted to be able to thank Him for giving me a hope where I had no hope, and a future where I had no future. But as that verse told us - HE had the plans, my part was to be open to act in faith upon them. I had sought Him with all my heart, and He had set me free from the captivity that was terminal cancer.

We were still keen on the idea that William had mentioned of using the flexibility that we had with the 8.30 service to have an opportunity for giving thanks. We recalled how one day during my illness William had been driving home following a visit to a patient as the local Hospital Chaplain. He remembered the story in scripture when Jesus had healed ten lepers (Luke 17:11-19). Despite the amazing miracle that He had worked in their lives, only one of them took the trouble to return and express their thanks to Him, but there was more to it than that. The cleansed leper had not only said, "Thank you", he had put himself at the Master's feet, in a place to receive whatever direction Jesus had for him. We felt that God was saying that we should be open to do the same.

Unknown to William, as I was sitting reading at that same time, I had the strongest feeling that when my healing was confirmed, whenever that might be, I wanted to have some kind of service of thanksgiving. When he arrived home I met him in the hall with the news of what I had felt, and when he shared the Scripture he had been given, we could see the direction we should go. At that time we had no idea when that day of healing might be, but we were believing in faith that it would surely come. Now it was here, and we picked a date for the service of thanksgiving – the "8.30" on Sunday the 25th of July 2004.

We weren't exactly sure how this would go, but we remembered the words of a speaker on TV one day – *"God doesn't look for your ability – he looks for your availability!"* It seemed to us that the best thing we could do is make ourselves available to Him, and leave the rest in His hands.

On the last day of our short break, we were visiting a beautiful place called Powerscourt House and Gardens near the village of Enniskerry, a village where the older boys had been in primary school when we lived in Bray. William took a call on his mobile from Louie, a lady in our Newcastle church, to say that her sister had died, and she was checking if he would be back in time to take the funeral service on Monday. He explained that we would be home that evening and would call with the family to make the arrangements.

Kathleen Mulligan was a lovely elderly woman of faith who had moved from Bangor to Newcastle to be near to her family. She hadn't been very well, and William had regularly visited with her both in hospital and at her daughters' home. She had always asked about me, and assured us of her prayers for my healing. Her funeral would be a joyful celebration of a life well lived, and would take place in two parts, first in Newcastle, and then it would travel quite a long way to a church near the original family home in County Tyrone.

When we arrived home we opened our mail, and discovered a letter which was from Kathleen, dated the 13th of July. It turned out to be the last letter that Kathleen had ever written. She wrote,

Dear William and Sharyn,

Praise God from whom all blessings flow. My heart is filled with joy and gladness. Gladys, Iris and I have just heard the great news of the Lord's healing touch, Sharyn, on your body. I have shed many tears – all now with joy and gladness. I now pray that many, as a result, may be moved to repentance, to accept the Saviour as Lord and Master. We continue to pray that God will give you strength to witness clearly. Praise God again and again!!

With my love, Kathleen

We were so grateful to Kathleen, writing in her fraility, and through the pain we know she had in her right hand. It felt like a message of encouragement directly from heaven, and we continue to treasure that letter today.

24

I HAVE MY LIFE BACK!

Early on Monday morning, William was preparing to go to the funeral when he made a quick phone call to Terence, the editor of our very popular local weekly newspaper, the Mourne Observer, which covers most of the area in and around South County Down. Whenever there were special services, such as Lent or Advent, most of the local churches would submit an advertisement to their special churches page. We had planned the Thanksgiving Service for the following Sunday, but the deadline for copy was 6pm on Monday. William knew that there was no way he could get it done by then as he would be engaged with the funeral all day, which would finish up 50 miles away, thus the call to ask if he could give the notice in on Tuesday morning instead.

"A Thanksgiving Service?" said Terence. "It's a bit early for harvest, isn't it! What's it about?!" He had heard that I hadn't been well, and when William told him briefly why we were having the service, he asked if we would be free the following morning to do a short interview. He said that he would like to send a reporter and photographer around to the manse as it was a good local interest story, and if he put it as a small article on the churches page with the details of the service at the end, then we wouldn't have to pay for the notice! It seemed like a good deal to William, so he agreed first, and told me afterwards!

On Monday we spent most of the day at the funeral, which was very moving, especially when William read out Kathleen's final letter. On Tuesday the doorbell rang and it was Neil Loughran from the Observer. It felt strange being interviewed by a reporter about what had happened to me, but Neil was a really nice guy, who put us very much at ease, and it seemed a good way to let the local community know what had been happening. The photographs were taken and they went on their way.

Early on the Wednesday morning we had a call from the Irish News, a newspaper that has a wide circulation in both Northern Ireland and the Republic of Ireland. They said it was regarding the front page story in the Mourne Observer, and they would like to do an interview about it. "Front page?" said William "Are you sure? We thought it was going on the local churches page!" Arrangements were made for the interview, and William dashed down to the local shop to get the paper.

As he walked into the shop, the first thing he saw was a large photograph of us on the front cover with the bold banner headline, "I HAVE MY LIFE BACK! – CANCER STRIKEN NEWCASTLE WOMAN TELLS HER REMARKABLE STORY." I was amazed when I saw it, but hardly had much time to read it before it was time to do the interview with the Irish News and then a photographer arrived for another photoshoot. The interviewer said it would probably go into a section they had on local interest stories, and we presumed that would be the case – it wasn't how that turned out either! The next morning, during their breakfast news programme just before 9am, BBC Radio did their usual "Review of the Papers" slot, and they finished by talking about what they called "a good news story for a change" – My story, about my Cancer recovery a "miracle", with a family photo, was now a headline on the front page of the Irish News.

Phone calls began flooding in from people who had read both articles, including one from Sarah Henry from Ulster Television, part of the ITV network. She wanted to take a camera crew out to our home and do an interview with us for UTV Live – a countrywide television news programme.

It was a beautiful sunny day, and they filmed the family in the garden of our home with the Mourne Mountains in the background. Sarah took some time to interview William and I about what had happened, but we were well aware that news can change in an instant, so we wouldn't have been too surprised if it hadn't appeared at all ... it did! That evening the programme began with what they call a "headline teaser" at 5.30 inviting people to hear about a "remarkable story of healing" – then they showed the whole interview in their prime-time slot, just before the six o'clock news. It was broadcast in full, and as we watched it we remembered the word I had received that I would share my healing with many people.

We took it that this was what the word meant. Now that people had read it in the papers, heard it on the radio, and seen it on TV, we would have our service of thanksgiving on Sunday and then get back to normal – but we had no idea the effect that all this media attention would have. God was at work – He wanted His truth to go forth, and it wouldn't end with the media.

On Sunday afternoon we went into the church to make some preparations for the evening. This was where the flexibility of the '8.30' came in very useful. Because it didn't have a rigid structure to it, people were never too sure what to expect when they came along. This might not have been a good thing in everyone's eyes, but for the most part the people who came appreciated it.

On a good summer evening in Newcastle with visitors, we might get about thirty to forty people coming along, twice as many as the fifteen or so on winter nights.

We put out a few extra Mission Praise books and William set up his guitar ready to lead the worship. We wondered if anyone would turn up, and with a prayer, left it in the Lord's hands.

We arrived back at the church just after 8 o'clock, and I was feeling a little nervous at the idea of standing up at the front when there might be a few visitors there. On the other hand, some praying friends had said that they would come along, and I was looking forward to having a chat with them in the new coffee bar we had just set up, following the service.

We had only walked in through the back door when Justyn came running to greet us, "Mum, Dad, the church is packed! We've run out of Mission Praise books, we've run out of seats, we've even run out of space!" Sure enough, when we came into the church, we couldn't believe our eyes. Every pew was full throughout the church, extra seats had been put along the aisles, up behind the communion rail, and even in the pulpit! There was just enough space for William to get to the lectern to welcome everyone and lead the worship. He couldn't even see or hear Corwyn on the piano through the crowd, but they managed to keep it together anyway!

I had been nervous enough at the idea of speaking in front of a few visitors, but now I was about to be surrounded by a whole sea of faces! I closed my eyes and let the words of the final song wash over me ...

Faithful One,
so unchanging.
Ageless One,
You're my rock of peace.
Lord of all, I depend on You ...

I call out to You
Again and again.

You are my rock in times of trouble.
You lift me up when I fall down.
All through the storm,
Your love is the anchor,
My hope is in You alone.

"Well, Lord," I prayed, "I'm calling out to you again, I can't do this on my own, please give me your peace, I'm depending on you alone."

William finished the song and we managed to squeeze through the small gap to swop places so that I could get up to share my story. Then an extraordinary thing happened. As I started to speak, my nervousness seemed to fade away, and instead that sense of peace welled up within me, a feeling very similar to the one I had while on that telephone interview with Renewal Solihull. I didn't realise it then, but now I know that it was God's anointing. And as that anointing flowed, the Holy Sprit began to work in the lives of the people packed into that church in a very special way.

When I had finished you could have heard a pin drop. William stood up and spoke about the work of Jesus on the cross for both our healing and our salvation, quoting from Isaiah 53:5,

"... He was wounded for our transgressions, he was bruised for our iniquities: the chastisement of our

peace was upon him; and with his stripes we are healed."

He invited anyone who didn't know the Lord to join with him in prayer and a large number of people raised a hand to indicate that they had made a first time commitment to Christ. This had never happened in the church before in such numbers, and we were both amazed.

It was lovely to see some people there who had been praying for me through my time of illness. Some, like Wendy, Dorothy and Sally had travelled over from one of our previous churches near Portadown, but so many of the people there had simply come in response to the media interest. Now they had met not only with a story of healing, but with the Healer himself – they had met with Jesus. We were so glad that we listened to the Lord as He had guided us into holding the service that evening. I had my life back, and it was wonderful to be able to share that life with others during the service.

As it turned out, there was a lot more to come.

25

LIGHT THROUGH THE WINDOW

William closed the service in prayer and we thought it would be nice to go to the door to say goodbye to the people, many of whom had travelled quite a distance to be there. We squeezed our way down the packed centre aisle to the foyer, and began greeting and thanking them for coming as they left. Sometimes they would stop for a while and hold my hand, saying how much it had meant to them to hear what the Lord had done in my life.

There were two or three ladies who shared their situation with me, and I asked them if they would like to go back into the church so that I could talk to them a little more. We had just set up the coffee bar a couple of weeks before so I said to William that I would go back in and speak to them, when he went on down to it.

That evening I received my first invitation to speak, when a lady asked me if I would come and share what had happened to me at a meeting in a Christian Holiday centre in Newcastle that Thursday evening. I was surprised that someone would want to hear me speaking again, but I agreed to go anyway, before I thought about it too much!

We said goodbye to the last people in the foyer, and walked back into the church to see a sight that we would never forget.

The first eight or nine pews at the front on each side were still full of people. Our Sunday school superintendent, Meta came down the aisle to meet us. "Why are all these people still here?" we asked. "They're all here waiting for prayer for healing!" she said.

We were amazed! This was something that we hadn't done in our church before. In fact, this was something we hadn't done anywhere before! Justyn went down to look after the coffee bar, and Meta said she would mind Olivia and bring them home later, so that freed us up to go and meet with the people.

It was new to us, but we listened to each person that was there and then prayed that they would know God's healing power in their lives, just as I had done.

Corwyn had stayed to play and some people sang quietly while waiting to come to the front for prayer. Earlier in the evening we had sung one of my favourite hymns, which we had at our wedding, and as we prayed it was one of the songs that he was playing quietly,

> *Praise, my soul, the King of heaven,*
> *to His feet thy tribute bring;*
> *ransomed, healed, restored, forgiven,*
> *evermore His praises sing.*
> *Alleluia! Alleluia!*
> *Praise the everlasting King.*

I had sung that hymn so many times before, but that evening, as His healing anointing was beginning to flow, those words came alive in my spirit. "Ransomed, Healed, Restored, Forgiven." We were praying these things into the lives of the people in the name of Jesus, trusting Him to do His work, even if we didn't quite know what we were doing!

At one stage I glanced up at the beautiful stained glass window at the top of our church. It shows the parable of the good Samaritan, at the top a flame and dove depicting the work of the Holy Spirit, and the words underneath,

"The spirit also healeth our infirmities."

I remembered sitting in the church one Sunday and noticing those words for the first time. As the sunlight from outside streamed through the window, it was as if it shone right into me, giving me hope, and helping me to establish His healing words in my heart. There were many Sundays when I looked at it for most of the service. Now as we stood just below the window, I prayed, "Lord, minister to these people the way you ministered to me. Let your Spirit heal their infirmities."

We stayed at the top of the church until every person there had received prayer, finishing close to 11.30pm. One of our circuit stewards, Alec Frew, was there until the very end. As he was locking up, he said that in the sixty years he had been a member of the church he had never seen anything like this. Then he told us that the church had been so packed that some people had to be turned away – there just wasn't room left to fit any more in!

"I don't think that we've got any choice but to do all this again next week!", he said. He was right! Although we had no idea of it at the time, we would have many healing services, praying late into the night with people. Not once did we have to close up the church ourselves before we left. Alec was always there, taping the services, talking to people, encouraging them and taking details to follow them up in prayer. We'll be forever grateful to Alec, Maureen, Meta and Corwyn for the support given to us as the ministry began to develop over the coming weeks and months.

The following Wednesday, when the Mourne Observer came out, it carried another family photograph and a follow-up story by Neil Loughran, headed "HUNDREDS GATHER TO HEAR SHARYN'S STORY", which described how people had come from all over the country and packed the church to capacity. He also told how a man living in Australia had read the story on their online edition, and called his mother in Northern Ireland to tell her to come to the service. Another man contacted us who had also read the article on the internet in Germany, to ask for prayer for a close family member.

It gave us an interesting insight into how small the world actually is these days, and how the media and the internet can be such a powerful tool in getting God's Word out to people who need it, no matter where in the world they may be. We would become even more aware of this in the months following.

Thursday evening came along and I arrived at the meeting to be met at the door by the lady who had invited me at the thanksgiving service. She explained that there would be a short time of singing and then I would be invited up to share my story, followed by a cup of tea. There would be no invitation given to come for prayer ministry. In the back of my mind I took note that if I was ever asked to speak at a meeting again, I should check out what the expectations would be, on both sides.

It was a lovely meeting and the folks were really nice, several of whom came and asked for prayer anyway. After a while a man came to me and said, "Do you remember me from Sunday evening – you prayed for me at the end of your thanksgiving service" I said that I had, and asked him how he was doing. "How am I doing?", he said, "I'm healed, that's how

I'm doing!" I nearly fell over. "Wow, that's great, praise the Lord!" I said. Inside, I was doing somersaults!

I could hardly take it in that the Lord had used me to bring healing to someone else. He explained that he had been suffering from great pain in his body which had even prevented him from sleeping for quite a few nights. He had seen my story in the newspaper, and prayed that he would be given the opportunity to come and hear it for himself. "I was so blessed when it turned out that I was going to Newcastle, and would be able to come to your service," he said. "I knew then that the Lord was going to do something special for me."

He went on to say that following the time of prayer ministry, he had slept right through the night, and woke up the following morning with no pain. He hadn't had any pain since. He thanked me, we both thanked the Lord, and I went home with a lot to think about!

When we got home, I picked up the Mourne Observer which was lying on the kitchen table, and read another part of the article which said,

> *"Speaking in front of so many people would be a daunting experience for most, but Sharyn was only too happy to share her story with those who might have felt that all hope was lost."*

That sentence really seemed to capture what it was all about for me. Yes, it had been daunting, especially as I had never been a public speaker, but if the Lord had called and equipped me to do it, then I needed to be available to Him, to give that hope to those who have none, to share his words such as those in Jeremiah 17:14,

> *"Heal me, O Lord, and I shall be healed; save me, and I shall be saved; for thou art my praise."*

I have been challenged and even cautioned on occasion not to give people 'false hope', but how can there be false hope when the only hope I point people to is in Christ? I didn't have hope in 'hope', and I didn't have faith in 'faith'. It definitely wasn't positive thinking.

No, my hope and my faith was, and is, entirely in the Lord Jesus, what He achieved for me on the cross by His precious blood, and what He is achieving through me now by His Holy Spirit.

It wasn't long before God began to open more doors, and provide more opportunities to share my story, as the article had said, to give real hope to those 'who might have felt that all hope was lost'.

That sort of hope is found in a song I really love called, "Stretch out your hand to Jesus" on an album by William's sister Vie Ewing. The lyrics, from an original poem by William's mother, point the way to the One in whom we find that hope, no matter how we might be feeling at the time ...

> *"... in sorrow or in joy,*
> *there's always One who cares*
> *Stretch out your hand to Jesus,*
> *You know He's always there*
> *You know He always cares."*

26

THE GREATEST MIRACLE

When Sunday evening came, the church was again packed with people who had travelled from all over Ireland for prayer for healing. We had asked Steven to bring along the Elim worship team, and they sang some of the Abundant Life worship songs that had meant so much to us. After we had both shared, we invited people to come to Christ, and again many prayed that prayer of commitment. This time we invited people forward for prayer as the worship continued, and again we were still praying at 11 o'clock.

When we were at the top of the church ministering with the last people we had noticed two couples sitting near the back on either side. We later discovered that one of them was Wesley and Frances Lindsay. They had been contacted by Pastor Dave who suggested they should come and see what the Lord was doing in Newcastle. They had been praying for us all evening, and would become some of our closest friends in our ministry.

The other couple were sisters-in-law, one of whom wasn't a Christian. She described how she had felt like leaving earlier on, but for some reason had been "stuck to her seat!" "I don't know what's happening to me," she said, "I've never felt this way before." We shared with her that it wasn't emotionalism, it was the Lord reaching out to her, and what she was feeling was an encounter with Him. I asked her if she would like to commit her life to Jesus and she said she would. I led her in prayer, and the tears rolled down all our cheeks as she followed me in a simple prayer of commitment, the first person I had ever personally led to the Lord. Her whole face had transformed in those few moments. In place of sadness and pain, there was a look of joy and peace.

Before we finished, she mentioned that she had been suffering with a very sore shoulder. I laid hands on her and prayed for healing, and then they left happily. A couple of weeks after that we found out that she had been off work with the pain in her shoulder for several months. They were together in her mother's home and the battery in the smoke alarm needed to be replaced. Without thinking, she reached up, opened the alarm cover with one hand, and replaced the battery with the other. Then she saw the look of surprise on the faces of her family. "How did you manage that?", they said, and she realised that her shoulder was completely healed! As that healing power was manifested in her life, it opened the door for her to share what had happened at the service and how she had given her life to the Lord. The following week she was able to return to work totally pain-free!

During the time that I had been ill, the Lord had told me on a number of occasions that I would be healed and share this with many people. Newcastle is a pretty small seaside town, and a few words in a local church, and in Café Crème over coffee would mean that everyone in the community would get to hear about what had happened to me in a couple of days at most!

I had thought that perhaps I might share my testimony in church once or twice. When the media picked up on the story, it became known to more people, and I assumed that was the fulfilment of the word that I had been given.

I certainly never expected what had happened over the past few weeks. Following the couple of services that we held, we were starting to get reports of many who had attended experiencing God's healing and saving power in their lives. Now people were asking when we would be holding another one. It certainly wasn't something we had planned to do.

We were amazed and delighted to hear about the healings, but by far the most pleasing reports were about the number of people who had given their lives to Christ.

Whatever miracle you may experience in your life as a result of healing prayer and standing on the Word of God, I would encourage you to realise that the greatest miracle of all is to know Him personally as your Lord and Saviour.

You could be reading this book at home, on a bus or train, in a hospital bed, on holiday – wherever you may be, God can speak to you, if you are prepared to listen to Him. He understands what you are going through, and He reaches out to you wherever you are. I don't believe in coincidence any more, only "God-incidents!". That you are reading this book right now is a God-incident in your life. I have known the Lord reaching out to me in places I would never have expected, from an MRI Scanning room, to a supermarket queue!

I mentioned earlier that on the Bank Holiday weekend following my bad news, I began to experience that frustration that perhaps you are going through right now, that feeling of frustration as the world is carrying on around you as normal. Perhaps you feel like crying out at the top of your voice, "Look at me - I'm sick, I'm hurting, I'm dying, why isn't anybody hearing me?", just as I did. But there is Somebody that hears your cry, and His name is Jesus.

One day I was in a supermarket queue with William, carrying on as normal, getting in the family groceries, and feeling just like that. He was actually packing the shopping, but he seemed to be miles away in his thoughts. When we got into the car, he turned to me and shared what the Lord had spoken into his life, there at the supermarket checkout!

> *"I can see your frustration now, but stand on my Word for your healing. Now think of the frustration you will feel when your healing is confirmed, and many will carry on as normal, ignoring my healing power. Now think of how it feels for a Father who sent His only Son to be the Saviour of a dying world – who shed his innocent blood on the cross for you and for many.*
>
> *"Feel how it feels for a loving Father, who saw His Son going through all that, so that His people could be ransomed, healed, restored and forgiven, and STILL they carry on as normal, as if nothing had happened – NOW you have a tiniest inkling of the pain of a loving Father."*

When we got home William talked about the words that the Lord had given to him, we turned to John 3:16, where we read together some familiar words,

> *"For God so loved the world, that he gave his one and only Son, that whoever believes in him, shall not perish but have eternal life."*

What amazing love our loving Father has for each one of us. I realised that if I had been the only one in this whole world, Jesus would have gone to the cross so that I could be forgiven of my sin, and healed of my sickness.

"He himself bore our sins in his body on the tree, that we might die to sins, and live for righteousness, by his stripes we were healed." (1 Peter 2:24)

The same is true of all of us. The greatest miracle of all in this world today is not being physically healed, it is being healed in our relationship with our loving heavenly Father, and being reconciled to Him, through His Son Jesus.

God's Word says,

"Behold, I stand at the door, and knock: if any man hear my voice, and open the door, I will come in to him, and will sup with him, and he with me." (Revelation 3:20)

Even as you read this page you can know this miracle in your own life. Perhaps I can help you by encouraging you to pray this prayer with me today.

Dear Lord Jesus,

I want to thank you that the greatest miracle of all is to know you as Lord and Saviour. I believe that you are the Son of God. I believe that you died for me on the cross and rose again.

I ask you now to forgive my sin and to cleanse me with your precious blood. I receive you as my Saviour and my Lord. Come into my heart right now and make me your child. I am yours, and you are mine. Thank you that I am born again. Fill me with your Spirit. Thank you that life will never be the same again. Amen!

If you prayed that prayer for the first time, you can be sure right now that you are a child of God, because you have taken a simple step of faith, and done what it says in His Word.

"... if you confess with your mouth the Lord Jesus, and believe in your heart that God hath raised him from the dead, you will be saved." (Romans 10:9)

You may feel that you have not had much to be happy about lately, perhaps that's why you're reading this book. But let me assure you that no matter what has happened, or will happen to your earthly body, you can be absolutely sure that you are going to heaven. and that you are safe forever in His loving arms.

Have no doubt about it - that's the greatest miracle of all!

27

THESE SIGNS SHALL FOLLOW

Following the second Thanksgiving Service we had been thinking about taking a short family holiday when we had a phone call from Pastor Dave in Solihull inviting me to come 'in person' and share at the two Sunday morning services in Renewal. We decided to combine the two and found ourselves 'checking in' at the home of the lovely Pete and Margaret Sizer, who not only show us wonderful hospitality when we come to Solihull, but also are a great encouragement for our ministry.

That Sunday, for the first time, we met Pastor Richard Taylor, a tremendously gifted evangelist, who has a truly amazing story of deliverance from a life of drugs and crime – he met with the Lord behind bars at Swansea Prison. He was taking the service, and as my story had been carried in the local newspaper that week, there were a number of additions to their usually full services. After I had shared my story, Richard invited me to pray over the many people who came forward for prayer in both meetings; again, this fresh anointing seemed to freely flow through me.

We were invited back for the Tuesday evening Ministry of Power meeting; it was especially emotional for me as I shared about the night back in June when I had been there myself. Pastor Dave asked me to pray for those who came forward; many people spoke to me afterwards who were in the same situation that I had been in. I felt that I knew exactly what they were going through and I encouraged them to believe God to work in their lives too. As we left later that evening I realised that over those few days I had spoken to thousands of people. I felt very privileged and blessed to have been used of the Lord to touch them in this way.

We enjoyed the rest of the break and wondered if things would settle down when we returned home to Newcastle. It wasn't to be, as we found lots of enquiries wanting to know when our next service was. I suppose we were quite staggered at the response. We were learning very quickly that the Lord was using us in a special way, but that didn't make us giants of faith overnight – far from it, as a couple of instances will illustrate!

Every summer for many years in Newcastle, Scripture Union CSSM (Children's Special Service Missions) had run holiday Bible clubs for children, and Olivia loved to go along with her school and Girls Brigade friends. One day, while playing in the garden at home, she had an accident and ended up in the Accident & Emergency Department of Downpatrick hospital with a badly twisted knee. An x-ray revealed that it wasn't broken, but they recommended total rest for the coming week. Olivia said, "Well, mum and dad, you could pray for it, you know!" We agreed it was a very good idea so we laid hands on her knee, and rebuked the pain and inflammation in Jesus' name.

On Monday morning she bounced down the stairs and into our room, shouting, "Jesus and God have healed me! When is CSSM starting?"

Of course, this great man and woman of faith had planned to keep her home to rest the knee as per doctor's instructions, so there was a mad scramble to get ready! She got there a little late, but enjoyed the whole week's activities, and has never had any bother with her knee since!

One day William was in the study on his computer making up a notice for our next service at the beginning of September when he came out to see me. "I'm struggling with this," he said. "We can't go calling it a Thanksgiving Service again, can we?" "No, I don't suppose we can," I replied. "Maybe we could call it a Healing Service?" "Yes, well, it did occur to me alright," he said, "but then I thought, if you call it a Healing Service, people have got to get healed! It's a risky thing to do, don't you think?" "Risky maybe, but faith-filled definitely," I said. We talked about it a little more and decided to go ahead and, in faith, call it a Healing Service.

If there was something we were sure about, it was this. During our ministry to date we had never prayed for healing for anyone, and so we had never seen anybody healed. As the opportunities had opened up and we had started praying for healing, we could see it flowing in the lives of the people who had gathered, and there didn't seem to be any good reason to stop now.

One of the concerns that we have always had is that people will often chase after the latest fads and fancies, as ministries come and go. We wanted to be absolutely sure that whatever we were doing was grounded on, and rooted in, the Word of God. After all, that's how my healing had come and the last thing we wanted was to encourage people to run around the place following signs and wonders, instead of following Jesus.

We began to search the Scriptures again, this time to see exactly what it was that Jesus said about the ministry which he expected to see manifested in the lives of those who would follow Him. It's been said that a person's last words may be the most important ones they ever utter, so we turned to Mark chapter 16 to see what some of Jesus' last words were on the earth to His disciples.

> *"And he said unto them, Go into all the world, and preach the gospel to every creature. He that believes and is baptised shall be saved; but he that does not believe shall be condemned. And these signs shall follow them that believe; In my name shall they cast out demons; they shall speak with new tongues; They shall take up serpents; and if they drink any deadly thing, it shall not hurt them; they shall lay hands on the sick, and they shall recover."* (verses 15-18)

There was the answer to our concern, we were to do exactly what Jesus said – to be those who believe. It's perfectly true that we shouldn't be following signs – as believers, signs should be following us!

If we were to take the Jesus at His word, we should be expecting these things to happen. In Acts 10 Peter told the people at the house of Cornelius that Jesus had come to preach peace, and that's a lot deeper than our understanding of the English word. The Hebrew word for peace is Shalom – it means "nothing missing, nothing broken".

That's what Jesus did in His ministry, as Peter said,

> *"... God anointed Jesus of Nazareth with the Holy Spirit and with power: who went about doing good, and healing all that were oppressed of the devil; for God was with him."* (verse 38)

Jesus still ministers to those who have broken hearts and broken lives, to those who are missing that peace that only a relationship with Him can bring.

Over the next few months, we began to have monthly Healing Services in Newcastle. Doors also opened for us to go and minister in many different places around Ireland, both North and South, and across the Irish Sea in England. As we stayed firmly rooted in the truth of the Gospel, we saw the Lord working in awesome ways. We began to get many reports of God's healing power at work.

Young Matthew was just under one-year-old when he started taking seizures, and had a trance-like look on his face which couldn't be explained. The following month he was referred for scans when the first one revealed lumps on his brain. Then he was referred for specialist care during which he had every scan possible over a two-week period. A biopsy was carried out and sent over to England for analysis. Much like my own situation, because it turned out to be very rare it was then sent to Toronto and California for further tests. They came back inconclusive; the symptoms persisted and worsened. No treatment was given and his parents were told that the lumps were getting bigger, giving great cause for concern.

During this time a man came forward at one of our services to tell us about his one-year-old grandson, Matthew. We prayed for him that night and he said that he would ask his family to come along to our next service with Matthew. They came, and then continued to bring him along to every Healing Service for prayer. After a period of time his scans started to improve and then, following a service on the 8th May, he had scans the following day. On the 12th the scan results revealed that the lumps which had been so aggressive had suddenly decreased. We continued to pray for him regularly and then in November his parents came to the top of the church excitedly clutching a letter from Matthew's consultant saying that the lumps had further decreased again considerably from his last scan, so much in fact, that they didn't need to see him again for another year. "Oh," they said, "did we tell you when they see Matthew coming they call him the 'miracle baby'!" His parents have no doubt at all that Matthew's wonderful recovery is down to the prayer received.

So is 'miracle baby' just a throwaway comment or an actual description of what has happened in young Matthews life? There's no doubt at all that Jesus did miracles and the people He encountered experienced 'instant' healing, although some like the blind man in Mathew 8:22-25 required further prayer before he could see perfectly.

In these days people find it very difficult to get their intellect around the idea that miracles can happen today. Up to a few years ago we would have thought that too! It was C. S. Lewis who wrote, "A miracle is an interference with nature by supernatural power." And that is what we have seen in action.

My own consultant, Aidan O'Brien, over a period of time progressed from telling me the devastating news that my condition was terminal to the wonderful news that my scans were completely clear, but he still would not be comfortable using the word 'miracle' about my case.

In our ministry we have seen people instantly healed, and we have seen people respond to continuous and persistent prayer. As I have mentioned before, we have never suggested to anyone that they should desist from seeking medical attention, and indeed it's worth pointing out that none of us have any problem going back to the doctor as many times as it takes to receive from them what we need by way of prescription and advice.

Shouldn't we give the Lord, at the very least, the same opportunity to work in our lives? Shouldn't we take His Word seriously and allow His healing words to work on us too?

"For they are life to all who find them, and health to all their body." (Proverbs 4:22)

I continue to take in the Word of God like medicine to my body, soul, and spirit every day of my life. If we get a prescription it's written on the bottle, "finish the course". I treat the Word just like that! As we are faithful to His Word, walking in it, and sharing it with others, so He is faithful to confirm it. I not only believe that He does this, I've seen Him do it, just as He did through the lives of the early disciples, and just as we should all expect Him to do today. We are reminded of this in the rest of the Mark 16 passage,

"So then after the Lord had spoken to them, he was received up into heaven, and sat on the right hand of God. And they went forth, and preached everywhere, the Lord working with them, and confirming the word with signs following." (verse 20)

28

SHOW ME!

The year 2005 was a momentous if unexpected one in terms of the progression of the ministry to which God had called us. Yet again we had expected that things might begin to slow down and we would settle into a pattern of having regular monthly healing services in our church in Newcastle. Instead, we became busier than ever, with my story again being picked up by the media, initially the Newsletter and the Telegraph in Belfast.

Speaking engagements, both in Northern Ireland and in England continued, but the most amazing thing for us was the number of people we saw coming to a living faith in Christ, as we saw the outworking of the promise that the Lord made to confirm the preaching of the Word.

The foot of the Mountains of Mourne can be a fairly quiet and peaceful location, but occasionally the skies over our home would buzz with the sound of helicopters. It was a sure sign that the highly skilled Mountain Rescue teams were being deployed as one of the many climbers or walkers that frequent the region found themselves in difficulty. In October 2004, Esther was airlifted to hospital following a nasty accident in the mountains. She had been on crutches and developed very severe sciatica.

One Friday in March 2005 she went to see her Chiropractor who sent her to the hospital A&E because the pain in her back was so bad. They gave her an MRI scan that afternoon and it confirmed that she had a slipped disc pressing on some nerves. In an email to us, she wrote,

> *"The good news was I did not need an operation, the bad news was there is no quick fix. I was told to take tablets and continue seeing the chiropractor."*

The following Sunday evening we were sharing at a service in Christian Fellowship Church in Belfast. It was a long night with lots of people coming for prayer and the very last one was Esther.

Her own words tell what happened next,

> *"I woke on Monday morning, rolled over onto my back expecting the pain to hit as it did every other morning ... and I'm still waiting! I am completely pain free and am doing things this week like picking things off the floor, turning over in bed, even putting on my socks ... with no pain! It's fantastic!! I had an appointment with my Chiropractor on Monday evening. She checked me over and told me that I was fine!! She was freaked ... it was really funny! Since then, I have had countless opportunities to tell people what God has done, which is just fab!"*

G.K. Chesterton once wrote,

"When people stop believing in God, they don't believe in nothing ... they believe in anything."

Whatever people may think, and whatever they may believe, we know by faith that these things are entirely down to the finished work of the cross, and for that we give Him all the glory.

I never cease to be amazed at the opportunities that have opened up in many avenues of life. One day an email arrived from a teacher who was writing a workbook for the school curriculum, the subject being "The Miracles of Jesus". Fiona had heard me being interviewed and wanted to know if she could use my story under the heading, "A modern-day miracle?"

I was happy to agree to it and so it was produced, with my story, questions for the students to ask, and our ministry website as a teacher's resource.

Another day I had a phone call from a doctor who is in charge of the medical training in some of the top hospitals in the country. Often medical students had come back from other countries such as Africa or India, where they had seen things happening that they couldn't explain medically and they wanted to respond to this as part of the training provided. He had heard my story through the media, and asked me to come and share my experience. I went along to Queens University, gave a lecture, and had a lovely time with the students, answering their questions and encouraging them in the great work they would be doing, while reminding them not to leave God out of the picture when it came to the healing process.

During the time of my illness, Mel Gibson's movie "The Passion" came out in the cinemas. Our son Andy is a total movie buff and probably owns shares in 'Empire' magazine by now, judging by the amount of them he has filed in his room!

He went to see the movie and William asked what he thought of it, and whether he should go and see it. "Well, dad," he said, "I would say that it's not a movie that you would *like* to see, but it's a movie that you *should* see, it's not an easy watch."

He was right! William went to see it and it wasn't an easy watch. However, it was just before Easter, and it certainly inspired him in his preaching. At a large joint Holy Week service in the Presbyterian Church, lots of people commented that it was one of the most powerful sermons that they had ever heard, especially when he hit the pulpit with a mallet!

Having said that, William was chatting with Trevor Kennedy on the phone, and they agreed that perhaps the movie hadn't had as much of an impact on them as they had expected. "Maybe it's because we spend time each Easter as ministers studying the subject, trying to get across to people what it was like, so that it wasn't that much of a surprise to us," he said, and William agreed, maybe that explained it. Now it was a year later, and "The Passion" had just been released on DVD.

Following a very good response to the Alpha Course, William had again teamed up with Pastor Peter from the Baptist Church, Pastor Steven from the Elim, and Rev Ivan from the Presbyterian. They hired the Newcastle Leisure Centre on Easter Sunday evening and through posters and the Observer, invited the whole community to come and see it. After the screening there would be a short address to give people an opportunity to respond to the message of the Gospel.

William had a joint service to do earlier in the evening in another part of the circuit, and so he slipped into his seat just as the movie was beginning. What he didn't expect was how watching it again would have such a deep effect on him.

As the opening music draws to a close, six words hang on the screen, "By His stripes we are healed". Suddenly the impact of those words hit William in a new and fresh way, and he began to think about all that we had gone through when I was ill, and how much those words had been, quite literally, life to me.

The film progressed, and came to the graphic depiction of Jesus' scourging and suffering at the hands of the Roman soldiers. "Those stripes were for Sharyn's sickness," he thought, as the tears flowed freely down his cheeks. "They are for everyone's sickness who call upon Him."

When he came home I could see that he had been deeply affected by what he had seen, and we turned to what the Amplified Bible said in Isaiah 53,

> *"Surely He has borne our griefs (sicknesses, weaknesses, and distresses) and carried our sorrows and pains [of punishment], yet we [ignorantly] considered Him stricken, smitten, and afflicted by God [as if with leprosy].*
> *"But He was wounded for our transgressions, He was bruised for our guilt and iniquities; the chastisement [needful to obtain] peace and well-being for us was upon Him, and with the stripes [that wounded Him] we are healed and made whole."*

What a powerful way the Amplified Bible puts it – my sickness, my weakness, my distress – Jesus had died for all of these things. There is so much more there than we had first understood. We looked up the word 'salvation', and found that it comes from the Greek word "Sozo," meaning deliverance, protection, healing, and to make whole.

William has always loved musicals, but none more so than My Fair Lady, no doubt because he appeared in a production of it once! At one point Eliza Doolittle is furious at the lack of love or emotion being shown to her, and she sings,

> *"Sing me no songs, rhyme me no rhymes,*
> *don't waste my time, show me."*

Jesus didn't just talk about loving us. He has showed us in His ministry and on the cross through His precious blood that was shed just how much He loved us. He is still showing this in the world today as He radically changes the lives of those who turn to Him, as we have seen many times. Just as John wrote in his letter,

> *"This is how God showed his love among us: He sent his one and only Son into the world that we might live through him."*

29

ALL THINGS ARE POSSIBLE

People have often asked me what part faith had to play in my
healing process and I can again only look to the Scriptures for
the answers to this. The writer of the book of Hebrews gives us
a whole chapter on the importance of faith, beginning with the
words,

> *"Now faith is the substance of things hoped for,
> the evidence of things not seen."*
> (Hebrews 11:1)

I long to bring people hope in the Lord, but it is faith that
adds substance to that hope, and it is by faith that we believe,
even when we do not see. I believe that faith is a choice that we
make. I have already said that faith comes by hearing, and
hearing by the Word of God, but we make the choice to expose
ourselves to that Word.

There's actually only one occasion when the Bible tells us that Jesus couldn't, not wouldn't do anything in a certain place, actually his home-town. Matthew tells us that,

"He could not do many miracles there, because of their unbelief." (Matthew 13:58)

Even with all that He had done, they could not see past the fact that, as far as they were concerned, He was a carpenter's son, and He could not give, because they would not receive.

We often go over to minister at one of the pastorates attached to 'Alpha' church, Holy Trinity Brompton in London. There we have made some really good friends including Joy, Bella and Anthony, and the leaders of the pastorate, Maggie and Andrew.

Andrew is a valuer of very fine art, and during one of our recent visits to minister there, William turned to him and asked which of the lovely pictures they had displayed on the wall was the most expensive. Without hesitation, he pointed to a particularly beautiful one, full of vibrancy and colour.

"Okay," said William, "I'll wrap that up in some old newspaper and bring it down to the church car boot sale tomorrow!" Andrew looked shocked. "You couldn't possibly do that!" he said. "Why not?" said William. "Why, it's worth a great deal of money," replied Andrew. "Just a moment now," enquired William, "what was your father's business?" "He was a farmer in Somerset," came the reply. "Well, then, that settles it," said William, "if I want to know about cows, I'll ask you, but what can a farmer's son possibly know about valuing fine art?!"

The point was made, and we could see how easy it was for people to choose not to believe what Jesus could do even when they had heard and seen Him do it. Of course, what they didn't consider at all is that He was actually going about His Father in heaven's business! Their pre-conceived ideas stopped the anointing from flowing, and we're told that Jesus himself *"marveled because of their unbelief"* (Mark 6:6).

I believe that the Lord responds to simple faith, which was the only kind I had. Sometimes people say to me, "Oh, you must have had great faith," or even, "You must have had great faith because you were a minister's wife!" That's not how it was at all!

I think of the time when Jesus encountered a man whose son was in serious need of help. He told him,

> *"... all things are possible to him that believeth. And the father of the child cried out, and said with tears, Lord, I believe; help thou mine unbelief."* (Mark 9:24)

I can understand how that man called out to Jesus through his tears, because I did that myself. I am sure that it is a cry He longs to hear from each of us, as we throw ourselves on His mercy and love when at the time of our deepest need. I would love to encourage you to do just that, cry out to Him, and be sure that He will put His loving arms around you. He will meet you where you are, just as He met with me. I have seen Him meet with many people at that place of need, sometimes when they least expected it.

As we encourage people to stand firm even in the face of fear and trust in the Lord, we remember the Braveheart word that William was given in Donegal, and we have seen freedom come into many lives in these days.

We were holding one of our now regular healing services in Newcastle and had seen a number of people respond to the appeal to commit their lives to Christ. Now as my friend Denise ministered on the piano in music and song, the invitation was made for people to come up to the front for prayer ministry.

We had just been praying with a young man who had a lot of problems in his life. He had been brought along by Ben, a young American missionary who was working with the Project Evangelism teams who were now helping us with our coffee bar outreach venture.

We had seen a big change take place in this young man even as we prayed, and we were thanking the Lord for that, but what happened next was truly wonderful.

There was a young mother (whose name I will not use to protect her privacy) sitting in an electric wheelchair in the aisle, and I had noticed that she seemed to be listening carefully to every word I said as I had shared my story.

Fours year earlier, William had been in his study in Portadown, and had a telephone call from another Methodist minister and his wife, in a different part of the country. They asked him if he would go and visit a friend who was in the local hospital, as she was very upset at being diagnosed with an aggressive form of Multiple Sclerosis, and was now using a wheelchair to get around. He had spent an hour with her offering a listening ear and a comforting prayer, which she had appreciated very much.

The MS had progressed as anticipated and for the previous year leading up to this service she had been in an electric wheelchair. As time went on the situation with her MS was so desperate and hopeless that her Consultant had been looking at some radical new treatment. Two weeks before that evening she was lying in her hospital bed asleep, when he woke her up and said, "I'm sorry, we had a consultation and decided that the treatment would not be suitable for your condition. We can't do anything more for you – you're going home tomorrow."

She was distraught at the news, and when discharged, she phoned the friends who had originally asked William to visit with her.

As her friend was listening to her, she walked into the study, and there on the desk was a copy of my story, which had been reported in the *Methodist Newsletter*. She suggested that she might come along to our next Healing Service and she agreed. "Well, I'd tried everything else," she said.

She came forward for prayer, accompanied by her mother, and told us a little of her story, and how she had been given a hopeless prognosis. Then she told me how, when I was actually sharing my story, she had started to feel power coming into her right leg, a sensation that she had not felt in years.

She showed William an encouraging text message from her friend which said that she believed she could be healed. William then took the mobile phone, walked back up to the top of the church, and placed it on the communion rail. "Now, we'll pray that exactly what that message said will happen," he said, "and then you'll go and get that phone yourself!"

We anointed her with oil, laid hands on her and prayed, and a feeling that she described as heat came all over her as the power of the Holy Spirit flowed through her body. After a few minutes of prayer, she suddenly turned to her mother and said "Who's tipping my wheelchair? Someone is tipping up my wheelchair" Those wheelchairs are extremely heavy, and tipping one up at all would have meant quite a lot of effort, but the fact was, as her mum confirmed, there was no one near it at all.

"Well, then," I said, "it's nothing to do with us, God is doing this work, and that's His power flowing through you."

"Yes," she said, "I need to get out of this NOW!" She and William pushed away the foot-rests, and she took William's hands and slowly stood up … then as William walked backwards and I continued to pray, she started to walk! When he made sure that she was steady enough on her feet, William let go off her hands and said "Okay now, go and get your phone."

Completely unaided, for the first time in years, she walked up to the communion rail and picked up her phone, then cried and laughed and hugged everyone she could. We were all in tears, and although she would by nature be a very shy person William managed to do a very quick interview with her to let others there know what she had been going through before this evening.

It was a struggle to get the heavy wheelchair back down the aisle to the front door of the church, but she said that there was no way she was getting back into it!!

The healing service went on with the level of faith through the roof! We continued in prayer, and then noticed an unusual thing beginning to happen in the body of the church. Usually as the ministry progressed people would leave after prayer, and the congregation would get smaller as time went on. This evening, no one wanted to leave, they wanted to stay and worship the Lord, not only that, but the numbers in the church actually began to grow.

We couldn't see what was happening outside. But Alec told us later that she had left her wheelchair with her mother, and started to run up and down with some of the young people we had prayed with earlier in the service including the one who had only just given his life to Christ.

It was a very pleasant Bank Holiday Sunday evening, and as the church is right on Newcastle Central Promenade, there were plenty of people to tell! What we observed inside the church were those who wanted to see what was happening coming in off the prom, and after a while William took the opportunity to share the gospel once more. In response to what they had seen, many of the new and regular folks who came to the services invited the Lord Jesus to become their personal Saviour for the first time.

One man said, "How can I not believe that there is a God of love and power after what I have seen in this place tonight?"

The following Thursday, Olivia was in her school assembly when the visiting speaker told the story of my healing and what had happened in our service that Sunday evening – and he wasn't even there!

Good news travels fast – GOD news even faster!

30

ONE YEAR ON!

During the rest of 2005, the good news of what the Lord had done in my life continued to spread, and we began to believe that perhaps He wanted us to become more available to Him for this growing ministry. There never seemed to be enough time to respond to all the needs that came along, although we had some wonderful help from Alec and Maureen, who would never hesitate to look after Olivia, often collecting her from school at short notice if we were delayed while travelling back from ministering to someone. Although we were very careful to make sure that the demands of the ministry didn't take us from her too often, she loved to go there, and enjoyed her drawing and painting lessons!

Alec in turn saw it as playing a part in this new ministry, which was running alongside the responsibility of running a circuit of three Methodist Churches. In one of our Quarterly Church leader's meetings, he observed that if the folks listened to my story, they would hear that I shared how the Lord had spoken to me, saying "I will heal you, and you will share this with many people." "William and Sharyn are responding directly to God's call on their lives," he said. "Sharyn has been wonderfully healed, and we have seen some amazing things happening in the healing services, they can't just go ahead and ignore it as if nothing had happened, you know!"

What he said was so true. We began to realise that things for us would never get 'back to normal' and our ministry together was taking a different direction. William loved the people to whom he was ministering, and the loss of some very dear elderly folk seemed to compound this feeling as the families were so much in appreciation of his pastoral care. We could see that we were going to have to make some difficult decisions, but we also realised that if God had brought us to this point, then He would make the way clear. The last thing that we wanted to do was step outside His will for our lives. We simply handed it all over to Him, and said, "Lord, if you open the doors, we will go through them, but it's up to you to open them."

In the meantime, I continued to be amazed at what God was doing in and through me, not least in the media. As we came to my 'one year' anniversary in June 2005, I had been asked to speak in Saint Anne's Cathedral in Belfast by Brother David Jardine, a lovely man of faith who has run the Church of Ireland Divine Healing Ministry for many years. I had spoken at a conference alongside him a few months before, and I liked the fact that he could see how important the concept of 'standing on the Word' is to my story - something that anyone can do.

By that I mean immersing oneself thoroughly in the Word of God, keeping it in your heart and mind at all times, as I have explained elsewhere in this book. Of course, we have to be careful with the use of 'Christian jargon' – when I used that expression with a reporter during an interview one day, he picked up a Bible from the coffee table and asked me if I literally put it on the floor and stood on it! I think he was going to ask me for a demonstration!

That night at the cathedral the BBC arrived to interview both myself and Brother David before the service began, for broadcast during the breakfast news the following morning. When we came out of the room and into the Cathedral there must have been about 700 people gathered, and when William gave the appeal at the end, he lost count after 50 of the hands that went up when invited to give their lives to Christ, and many came for healing prayer.

Following the broadcast of my interview during the news the next morning, the telephone rang. It was a researcher from the Stephen Nolan television phone-in show, Nolan Live. I knew by now that Stephen's radio and TV shows had become very successful, not least because he has cultivated a reputation for being a hard, no-nonsense but honest interviewer, so I wondered what they had in mind The researcher said that they were doing a feature about 'healing' and asked if I would come on to sit in the audience and share my story if called upon. It seemed safe enough, so I said that I would and on the Wednesday evening we arrived at the BBC studios in good time.

A woman met us at the door and showed me to a dressing room with my name on the door. "That's strange," I thought, "How come my name's on the door, they hardly have that many dressing rooms that they give one to every member of the audience!" A few minutes later another girl came in. "Hello Sharyn, make-up in five minutes, okay?" "Sure, okay" I said, with what William describes as a bemused look on my face! I can't say that I was going to object to a nice make-over anyway, even if they had got me mixed up with somebody else! They hadn't!

The producer came in then and introduced herself. "You'll be sitting beside Stephen," she said, "then we'll have Dr Cecil Stewart beside you, Dr David Cerullo on a live satellite link from the USA, and another chap who has his doubts about these healing ministries!"

Twenty minutes later we were about to go on, and I was chatting with Cecil Stewart, whom I had gotten to know over the previous few months; Cecil and his wife Evelyn minister through the media with CCN, and also travel extensively in Africa and Ireland preaching the gospel.

As I listened to the countdown to "live on air", I thought about the verse which says,

"They overcame him by the blood of the lamb, and by the word of their testimony." (Revelation 12:11)

"Well," I prayed, as the opening credits rolled, "You have put me here Lord, I'm no theologian when it comes to hard questions, but I do have my testimony, and even if it only gives hope to one person watching, it will be worth it." The programme certainly generated response, with lots of phone calls, and they seemed pleased at the party they were having in the Green room afterwards, as it was the last in the series.

I met Stephen there 'face to face' for the first time, and we remembered the radio interview he had done with me the previous September. "I'm still here, Stephen," I said, and we both laughed.

He comes across on air as a hard man, and that's the style that has made him successful – off air, I found him to be a nice, charming guy.

The result of that show was that we had many more people coming along to our healing meetings, and contacting us by telephone and through the website which meant the ministry continued to grow, as we did a series of services through the summer and the rest of 2005 called "One year on! - A celebration of healing."

We continued to see God's healing power working in people's lives, including Helen, whose mum and dad first came for prayer for her when her prognosis with cancer was bad. She then came along with them regularly and persistent prayer brought healing to her body. Her dad John phoned me on New Years Eve to say that she was having a party for lots of kids in her home, which was great considering how ill she had been the first time that we had met, earlier in the year.

It was a very moving moment when the young mum who had been healed of MS the previous May Bank Holiday walked to the microphone to give her testimony, and when Rosemary celebrated her own "one year on", giving testimony to complete and instantaneous healing from fybromyalgia and severe depression in October 2004. Our website was getting more hits than we had ever anticipated when it was first set up. At that time we had decided to take advantage of our son Kelvin's amazing comptuer skills and as we came up with ideas, he had the ability to translate them onto the screen. One thing that we didn't have was a name for the site, and William tried to think up a few. I remembered the words of Psalm 91:16,

"With long life will I satisfy her
And show her my salvation."

"I like that," I said, "Long Life!" A search on the internet showed that it didn't appear to have been used before so, "Long Life Ministries" was born - but we never expected it to be any more than a name on a website at that time!

One Friday our friends Wesley and Frances rang to say that they had organised a meeting in their home where a man called Michael Ross Watson would be the speaker. A few years before he had been diagnosed with cancer himself and was feeling very down. Then, on an aeroplane he read a book by Derick Bingham called, 'Don't wait to praise him (until you're dead!)'. It inspired faith in him, and he prayed, "Lord if you heal me of this, I will serve you for the rest of my life." Many years on, the Lord is still using him throughout the Far East in ministry.

It was very informal, and Michael simply shared what the Lord had put on his heart. We know now that the evening was by God's design, and the Lord spoke deeply to us about our future, through Michael. That group would become a very significant part of our developing ministry.

Together with all the other guidance we had been given, it was clear to us that the time had come to step out into a fulltime ministry that we had never expected to have. We had trusted the Lord to open the door, and now that He had done so, we had to go through it.

In time, William resigned from the Methodist ministry and at the end of 2005, we moved as a family to Bangor, County Down. It was like coming home for us, as Olivia had been born there, and we had already done some Healing Meetings organised by Brian Ashworth in a local hotel, to which there had been a good response.

Never ones to miss a story the *Mourne Observer* printed an article with an interview, with the bold if mildly embarrassing headline, "MIRACULOUS MACKAYS BID FAREWELL TO NEWCASTLE!"

The *Daily Mirror* newspaper then ran my story throughout their whole network in December, followed by Womans Own magazine who carried it in their Christmas/New Year edition.

As a result of these articles many more people contacted us in our new location and Long Life Ministries was firmly established, where we are trusting the Lord for His guidance in days to come.

3 1

THE BEGINNING ...

When I had finished writing my healing journal in July 2004, I put two simple words on the last line – The End. One day I took it out of the drawer to take a look through it, and much to my surprise, I saw that William had crossed them out and replaced it with two words of his own – The Beginning! That's why I have put that title on the last chapter of this book – it has been the beginning of a whole new life for me, and my family; to bring the good news of the life of Jesus to others is an amazing privilege for both of us.

The great evangelist D L Moody captured it so well,

"Oh, the blessed privilege to be used of God to win a soul to Christ, and to see a man or woman being led out of bondage by some act of ours toward them. To think that God should condescend to allow us to be co-workers with Him. It is the highest honor we can

*wear. It surpasses the joy of our own salvation, this
joy of seeing others saved."*

Sometimes people ask me if I could sum up in a word what
has changed in my life since all this has happened and my reply
is – compassion. Jesus had compassion for all whom He met –
His passion was born out of compassion.

*"When Jesus landed and saw a large crowd, he had
compassion on them and healed their sick"* (Matthew
14:14). (See also Matthew 15:32; Matthew 20:34;
Mark 1:41)

Whenever I read an email, take a telephone call, stand up
to speak or minister in prayer, my heart breaks afresh for the
person receiving ministry every single time. I feel that
compassion welling up inside me. I weep for those who are sick
and in pain, whether in body, mind or spirit. I weep for those
who suffer loss, and I weep for those who don't know Jesus as
Lord.

As we have been writing this book, it has been a time of
re-living so much that has happened in my life, both bad and
good, and I pray that as you have walked this path with me, that
you will find the One who gave me hope and brought me
through.

*You are the Voice of Hope,
The Anchor of my soul;
Where there seems to be no way,
You make it possible.
You are the Prince of Peace,
Amidst adversity,
My lips will shout for joy,
To you the Most High.*

As you consider these words that meant so much to me, may I encourage you right now, whatever your situation might be, to take time to be still before God.

Rid yourself of any bitterness, resentment, or unforgiveness towards others, or even towards yourself.

Be reconciled to your family and friends, but most of all be reconciled to God.

Read and believe for yourself what He says in His word, and most of all in the midst of your storm, listen for the still small voice of calm, listen for the voice that I heard, the only one who could and did deliver me in my deepest time of need.

I pray that you will hear it today ...

It is the voice of Jesus,
It is the Voice of Hope.

With long life will I satisfy her and show her my salvation.
Psalm 91:16

You can contact William & Sharyn
via their website

www.longlifeministries.org